HSPT

Prep Book 2024-2025

for Catholic Schools

Essential Techniques and Insights for Top Scores.

Comprehensive Reviews and Practice Exercises

By

Leo Baxter

TABLE OF CONTENT

CHAPTER 1: NAVIGATING THE HSPT LANDSCAPE

Purpose of the HSPT:

The High School Placement Test (HSPT) is more than just an academic assessment—it's a critical filter used by Catholic high schools to determine the best candidates for their unique educational environment. The HSPT serves not only to evaluate the current academic achievements of students but also to predict their potential success in a demanding high school curriculum. By requiring this test for entrance, Catholic schools ensure that they are considering students who are prepared to meet the academic and spiritual rigor that is characteristic of Catholic education. It's an essential step in the admissions process, designed to align students' capabilities with the schools' standards of excellence.

Structure of the HSPT:

The High School Placement Test (HSPT) is methodically structured to assess a broad range of skills and knowledge that are pivotal for success in Catholic high school education. Its comprehensive design is broken down into five primary sections, each focusing on a specific academic area. Understanding the intricacies of each section is crucial for effective preparation and ultimate success on the test.

Verbal Skills Section: This section is designed to evaluate the student's command of the English language. It typically includes questions related to synonyms and antonyms, which test vocabulary strength; analogies and logic puzzles, which assess reasoning and critical thinking skills; and classification exercises, which require students to group words or concepts logically. This section is pivotal in determining a student's verbal reasoning and comprehension abilities, skills that are essential for all subjects in a high school curriculum.

Quantitative Skills Section: Targeting numerical ability, this section delves into mathematical reasoning and problem-solving skills. It includes a variety of question types such as number series, geometric and non-geometric comparisons, and arithmetic calculations. This section doesn't just test the student's knowledge of numbers but also their ability to apply mathematical concepts to solve practical problems, reflecting the analytical skills needed in high school mathematics.

Reading Section: Here, the focus shifts to reading comprehension. Students are presented with a variety of passages, ranging from narrative to expository texts, and are asked questions pertaining to the main idea, supporting details, inferences, and vocabulary in context. This section tests the student's ability to quickly and accurately understand, analyze, and interpret written material, a skill that is invaluable across all academic disciplines.

Mathematics Section: More comprehensive than the quantitative skills section, this part of the test includes questions on a range of topics from basic arithmetic operations to more complex algebra and sometimes introductory geometry. Questions are designed to assess a student's grasp of mathematical concepts and their ability to apply these concepts in different scenarios. This section is critical for determining a student's readiness for the math curriculum in Catholic high schools, which often includes advanced coursework.

Language Section: Focusing on grammar and usage, this section tests the student's understanding of English language mechanics. It includes questions on parts of speech, sentence structure, punctuation, and capitalization. The language section is essential in evaluating a student's written communication skills, which are fundamental for success in all areas of study.

Each section of the HSPT is timed, adding an element of pressure that tests the student's ability to efficiently manage their time while maintaining accuracy in their responses. The number of questions and the time allotted for each section can vary, but the test is usually designed to be completed in a few hours.

Scoring System:

The scoring system of the High School Placement Test (HSPT) is a crucial aspect for students to understand, as it plays a significant role in how their performance is evaluated and interpreted by Catholic high schools. The HSPT is typically scored on a scale, with each section of the test contributing to a composite score. This composite score is the primary metric used by schools to assess overall academic ability and readiness.

Section Scores: Each section of the HSPT – Verbal Skills, Quantitative Skills, Reading, Mathematics, and Language – is scored separately. The scores for these sections are determined based on the number of correct answers, with no penalty for incorrect responses. This means that guessing an answer is better than leaving a question blank. Understanding the scoring method for each section allows students to strategize their approach, especially in areas where they might be stronger or need more improvement.

Composite Score: The composite score is calculated by combining the individual scores from each section. This score is often the first aspect that admissions officers consider, as it provides a quick overview of a student's general performance across all areas of the test. A high composite score can be a strong indicator of a student's overall academic ability and readiness for high school level work.

Percentile Ranks: In addition to raw scores, students are often given percentile ranks. These ranks compare a student's performance to that of a norm group – typically a national sample of students who have taken the test in previous years. For example, a percentile rank of 75 means that a student scored as well as or better than 75% of the students in the norm group. This ranking helps to contextualize the student's performance in a broader scope.

Stanines: Another common measure used in HSPT scoring is the stanine score, which ranges from 1 to 9. This score is a simplified way to understand where a student falls within the normal distribution of scores. A stanine score of 5 is considered average, while scores closer to 9 indicate higher performance, and those closer to 1 indicate areas needing improvement.

Score Reporting: Scores are usually sent directly to the schools to which a student is applying. Some schools may also provide the scores to students and parents. It's important for students and parents to review these scores carefully, not only to understand the student's performance but also to identify areas that may need additional focus in future academic work.

Use in School Placement: Apart from admissions, these scores can also be used by schools for course placement. For instance, a high score in the Mathematics section could place a student in an advanced math class.

Study Plan Strategy:

A strategic study plan is indispensable for conquering the HSPT. Beginning with a diagnostic test offers a baseline, helping students understand their starting point relative to the test's requirements. From this foundation, a structured study plan can be developed, one that allocates time judiciously between reviewing material and honing test-taking skills through practice. The balance between learning new content and reinforcing existing knowledge through repetition is key to deepening understanding and boosting recall speed during the actual test.

Approach to Test Taking:

Academic knowledge is only one part of the equation for success on the HSPT. Equally important is the ability to apply this knowledge under the pressure of time constraints. Effective test-taking strategies include time management, question analysis, and an approach for guessing intelligently when uncertain. Building these skills is critical and requires practice under conditions that simulate the actual testing environment. By doing so, students can improve their efficiency and accuracy, turning potential stress into a performance advantage.

Encouragement and Direction:

At the heart of this chapter is a message of support and motivation. The journey to mastering the HSPT can be daunting, but with this guide, students do not walk alone. By breaking down the test's format and requirements, students are equipped with a map to navigate their preparation journey. Understanding the test's layout and what is expected brings clarity and focus to the study process. This initial step of grasping the test's fundamentals is a leap towards the larger goal—successful admission into a Catholic high school and the bright future that follows.

CHAPTER 2: MASTERING VERBAL SKILLS

This chapter is designed to guide you through the intricacies of enhancing your vocabulary, mastering analogies, and becoming adept at sentence completion - all crucial components of the verbal section. This journey is not just about memorizing words; it's about cultivating a deeper understanding of language and its nuances.

Enhancing Vocabulary: Building a Robust Lexicon

Vocabulary is the cornerstone of verbal proficiency. The HSPT tests your ability to understand and utilize a wide array of words. To excel in this area, it's essential to build a robust and varied vocabulary.

Word Lists and Flashcards: Expanding Your Vocabulary

To effectively build your vocabulary for the HSPT, begin with specially curated word lists. These lists are compiled based on the frequency and pattern of words appearing in past HSPT exams. Each list will introduce you to a range of words, from those commonly used to the more challenging ones that often appear in the test.

- **Creating Effective Flashcards:** For each word, create a flashcard. On one side, write the word, and on the other, its definition, synonyms, and antonyms. Also, craft a sentence that uses the word in context. This technique helps in understanding not just the meaning of the word, but also its practical application.

- **Regular Review Sessions:** Dedicate time each day to review your flashcards. This regular exposure is crucial for retention. Shuffle the cards to ensure you're not memorizing them in order, which helps in recalling the words independently.

- **Interactive Learning**: Engage with these words actively. Use digital flashcard apps that employ spaced repetition techniques to optimize your learning and retention of these words.

Reading Widely: Cultivating a Rich Vocabulary

Broadening your reading horizons is an effective and enjoyable way to enhance your vocabulary. Diverse reading materials expose you to a variety of words, styles, and contexts.

- **Novels and Literature:** Fictional works often use rich, descriptive language, offering a fun way to encounter new words. Historical novels or literature can be particularly useful due to their diverse and sometimes archaic vocabulary.

- **Newspapers and Journals:** Regular reading of newspapers and academic journals introduces higher-level language and specialized terms, which are invaluable for expanding your vocabulary.

- **Incorporating New Words:** As you read, make a habit of noting down unfamiliar words. Look up their meanings, and then try to use these new words in your daily conversations or written assignments. This active use of new vocabulary aids in cementing these words in your memory.

- **Diverse Genres:** Don't limit yourself to just one type of reading material. Explore various genres and formats, including essays, biographies, scientific articles, and poetry. Each genre offers a unique set of vocabulary and a different way of using language.

Roots, Prefixes, and Suffixes: Decoding Words

Understanding the roots, prefixes, and suffixes of words is akin to having a toolkit that can unlock the meaning of numerous words.

- **Learning Common Roots:** Start by learning common Latin and Greek roots since many English words are derived from these languages. For example, knowing that 'bene' is the Latin root for good, as in 'benevolent', helps you understand related words like 'beneficial' or 'benefactor'.

- **Prefixes and Suffixes:** Similarly, familiarize yourself with common prefixes and suffixes. For instance, the prefix 'un-' denotes 'not', as in 'unhappy' or 'uncertain', while the suffix '-ful' suggests 'full of', as in 'hopeful' or 'joyful'.

- **Building New Words:** Practice combining these roots, prefixes, and suffixes to form new words. This not only helps in understanding words you might encounter but also allows you to confidently deduce the meanings of words you haven't seen before.

- **Practical Application:** Use exercises and quizzes to apply your knowledge of roots, prefixes, and suffixes. This active engagement helps in reinforcing what you've learned and makes word learning a dynamic process.

Complementary Flashcard App: Enhancing Your Study Experience

The paperback version of this HSPT guide includes access to a complementary flashcard app, which is a dynamic tool designed to make your vocabulary building more effective and engaging.

Remember, the key to expanding your vocabulary is not just about what you study, but how you study. By utilizing this flashcard app, you're not only learning new words, you're also learning them in a way that is tailored to your individual needs and learning style. This tool is more than just a supplement to your paperback guide; it's a powerful component of your overall preparation for the HSPT.

Mastering Analogies: Connecting Concepts

Understanding and solving analogies is a critical skill in the Verbal Skills section of the HSPT. Analogies are not just about word pairs; they are about the relationships between these pairs. Mastering this section requires a keen eye for detail and a deep understanding of how words can be related to each other.

Identify Relationships: The Key to Analogies

- **Types of Relationships**: The first step in mastering analogies is to recognize the type of relationship between the word pairs. Common relationships include synonyms (words that mean the same thing), antonyms (words that have opposite meanings), part to whole (where one word is a component of the other), function (what something does), and degree (variation in intensity or size). For instance, in the analogy "finger is to hand as toe is to foot," the relationship is part to whole.

- **Contextual Clues**: Sometimes, understanding the context in which words are used can provide hints about their relationship. Words might be related in terms of their function, their position, or their significance in a particular setting.

- **Consistency in Application:** After identifying the relationship in the first pair, the next step is to apply the same relationship to the second pair. Consistency is key here. The relationship that holds for the first pair must be true for the second pair for the analogy to be correct.

Practice Regularly: Building Analogy Skills

- **Diverse Exercises:** Engaging in a variety of analogy exercises is crucial. This can include worksheets, analogy sections from past HSPT exams, and online resources. Diverse practice helps you encounter a wide range of word relationships, preparing you for whatever the test might throw your way.

- **Timed Practice Sessions:** Since the HSPT is a timed test, practicing under timed conditions is essential. This not only helps you get used to the pressure of the exam but also improves your speed and accuracy in identifying relationships.

- **Creating Your Own Analogies:** A unique way to deepen your understanding is to create your own analogies. This exercise forces you to think about different types of relationships and how words can be connected. It's a creative and effective method to reinforce your learning.

- **Group Study Sessions:** Discussing and solving analogies in a group can be beneficial. It exposes you to different perspectives and explanations of how others understand and solve analogy problems. This collaborative learning can often provide new insights and enhance your comprehension.

- **Regular Review:** Regularly revisiting analogy concepts and practice questions is important for long-term retention. Just like vocabulary, analogy skills are honed over time with continuous practice and review.

Sentence Completion: Understanding Context and Meaning

Sentence completion questions on the HSPT are designed to assess your ability to interpret a sentence's meaning and to select the word or phrase that best completes it. These questions require a strong grasp of vocabulary and an ability to deduce meaning from context.

Context Clues: Deciphering Sentence Meaning

- Identifying Key Words: Words such as 'although', 'since', 'consequently', and others like them are pivotal in determining the direction of a sentence. They can indicate contrast, cause and effect, or a continuation of a thought. For instance, the word 'although' might introduce a contrast or exception to what was previously stated.

- Understanding Sentence Flow: The overall flow of a sentence can provide hints about what type of word is needed to complete it. Is the sentence building towards a specific point, contrasting an idea, or describing a cause-and-effect relationship? This understanding is crucial in choosing the right word.

- Inference Skills: Sometimes, the missing word is not directly stated, but can be inferred from the context. Developing the skill to infer meaning from the given information is key to mastering sentence completions.

Process of Elimination: Narrowing Down Choices

- Eliminate Obviously Wrong Answers: Start by eliminating choices that are clearly incorrect. This may be due to the meaning of the word or because it does not fit grammatically into the sentence.

- Consider All Answer Choices: Do not rush to select an answer after finding one that seems to fit; evaluate all options. Sometimes, a better choice is available that fits the context more accurately.

- Look for Trap Answers: Be aware of trap answers that might seem correct but do not quite fit the context or the grammatical structure of the sentence. These are often included to test your understanding of the sentence as a whole.

Practice Sentences: Sharpening Skills through Practice

- Diverse Practice Materials: Utilize various practice materials, including HSPT prep books, online resources, and past exam papers. This variety will expose you to different sentence structures and contexts, broadening your experience.

- Timed Practice: Since time management is crucial in the HSPT, practice completing sentences under timed conditions. This will help you get used to the pace needed during the actual test.

- Self-Creation of Sentences: Try creating your own sentence completion questions. This exercise challenges you to think about how sentences are constructed and what makes a word or phrase the right fit.

- Review and Reflection: After completing practice sentences, take the time to review your answers, especially the incorrect ones. Understanding why an answer was wrong is just as important as knowing why another was right.

Exercises for Skill Enhancement

Exercise SET 1:
Vocabulary Quizzes

1. Multiple-Choice Quiz:

Word: Ambiguous

- Obvious
- Doubtful or unclear
- Joyful
- Ancient

Word: Benevolent

- Malevolent
- Indifferent
- Kind-hearted
- Powerful

2. Word Usage Task:

In an act of (**generosity, ambiguity, tension, perplexity**), the philanthropist donated a large sum to the charity.

3. Synonyms and Antonyms Challenge:

Word: Prodigal

- Synonym: _____
- Antonym: _____

4. Analogy Challenges

Identifying Relationships:

Whisper is to Yell as Murmur is to _____.

- Talk
- Shout
- Silence
- Laugh

Completing Analogies:

Book is to Reading as Fork is to _____.

- Cooking
- Eating
- Cleaning
- Writing

5. Sentence Completion Tasks

Fill-in-the-Blank:

Despite the _____ evidence, the detective was able to solve the case with remarkable intuition.

- ambiguous
- plentiful
- direct
- insignificant

Creating Your Own Sentences:

The scientist's theory, though _____ at first, was later proved with substantial experimental data.

- confirmed
- controversial
- accepted
- undeniable

SET 1 ANSWERS:

Vocabulary Quizzes:

Ambiguous - B) Doubtful or unclear

Benevolent - C) Kind-hearted

generosity

Prodigal

- Synonym: Extravagant
- Antonym: Frugal

Analogy Challenges:

B) Shout

B) Eating

Sentence Completion Tasks:

A) ambiguous

B) controversial

Exercise SET 2:
Vocabulary Quizzes (Continued)

1. Multiple-Choice Quiz:

Word: Infallible

- Flawless
- Weak
- Fallible
- Unreliable

Word: Exacerbate

- Alleviate
- Worsen
- Calm
- Simplify

2.Word Usage Task (Continued):

The movie's plot was so (**convoluted, precise, direct, simple**) that many viewers found it hard to follow.

3.Synonyms and Antonyms Challenge (Continued):

Word: Elucidate

- Synonym: _____
- Antonym: _____

4.Analogy Challenges (Continued)

Identifying Relationships (Continued):

Author is to Book as Composer is to _____.

- Symphony
- Instrument
- Painting
- Poem

Completing Analogies (Continued):

Fire is to Hot as Ice is to _____.

- Cold
- Wet
- Hard
- Transparent

5.Sentence Completion Tasks (Continued)

Fill-in-the-Blank (Continued):

The politician's speech was so _____ that it appealed to a wide range of people, irrespective of their age or background.

- divisive
- convoluted
- persuasive
- monotonous

Creating Your Own Sentences (Continued):

To everyone's surprise, the _____ solution to the complex problem was suggested by the new intern.

- ineffective
- intricate
- simple
- problematic

SET 2: ANSWERS

Answers :

Vocabulary Quizzes:

4. Infallible - A) Flawless

Exacerbate - B) Worsen

convoluted

Elucidate

- Synonym: Clarify
- Antonym: Obscure

Analogy Challenges:

3. A) Symphony

A) Cold

Sentence Completion Tasks:

3. C) persuasive

C) simple

CHAPTER 3: QUANTITATIVE SKILLS DECODED

This chapter is dedicated to demystifying the concepts of arithmetic and basic algebra, focusing on enhancing your problem-solving abilities, your grasp of numerical logic puzzles, and your skills in quantitative comparison. Our goal is to transform these topics from daunting challenges into manageable and even enjoyable puzzles.

Understanding Arithmetic and Basic Algebra

"Core Arithmetic Skills" refers to the foundational knowledge and abilities in basic arithmetic operations, which are essential for proficiency in quantitative skills. These operations include addition, subtraction, multiplication, and division. A solid grasp of these skills is crucial not only for the HSPT but for mathematical problem-solving in general. Let's break down what each of these entails and how they form the core of quantitative skills:

Addition: This is the most fundamental arithmetic operation, involving the combination of two or more numbers to get a total or sum. It's the first building block of arithmetic and serves as a basis for more complex calculations. Mastery of addition includes being able to quickly and accurately add numbers of varying sizes, from single digits to multiple digits.

Subtraction: This operation involves taking one number away from another to find the difference. It is essentially the inverse of addition. Proficiency in subtraction is key for many mathematical tasks, including balancing equations and calculating changes in values.

Multiplication: Often described as repeated addition, multiplication is a faster way to add the same number several times. It is a critical operation for many areas of math, including algebra. Quick and accurate multiplication skills can greatly enhance your ability to handle more complex mathematical problems.

Division: This operation is the process of dividing a number into equal parts, essentially the inverse of multiplication. Understanding division is vital for fraction work, proportions, and various real-world applications like calculating averages or rates.

In revisiting these fundamentals with a fresh perspective, the aim is to move beyond mere understanding to achieving efficiency and speed. This involves:

Learning Shortcuts: There are numerous tricks and shortcuts that can simplify these basic operations. For example, understanding the patterns in multiplication tables, or using techniques like 'borrowing' and 'carrying over' in addition and subtraction.

Strategies for Quick Calculations: Developing strategies to perform these operations quickly and accurately is crucial, especially under timed test conditions like the HSPT. This might include mental math techniques, estimation for quick approximations, and recognizing common calculation errors to avoid them.

Applying Operations in Varied Contexts: It's also important to know how to apply these operations in different types of problems. This could mean recognizing when to use multiplication instead of repeated addition, or how to break down a complex problem into simpler arithmetic steps.

Overall, reinforcing core arithmetic skills involves more than just being able to do basic calculations; it's about doing them quickly, accurately, and knowing when and how to apply them effectively in various problem-solving scenarios. These skills form the bedrock upon which more advanced quantitative concepts are built.

Problem-Solving Techniques

Effective problem-solving in mathematics involves more than just arriving at the correct answer; it requires a deep understanding of the process involved in reaching that answer. Let's delve deeper into the two key techniques highlighted: the Step-by-Step Approach and Breaking Down Complex Problems.

Step-by-Step Approach

- **Understanding the Problem:** The first step is to fully understand the problem at hand. This means reading the problem carefully, identifying what is being asked, and noting any key information or constraints.

- **Devising a Plan:** Once you understand the problem, the next step is to plan how to solve it. This may involve choosing the right mathematical operation or formula, deciding the order of steps, or considering multiple approaches to see which one is more effective.

- **Implementing the Solution:** After planning, you start solving the problem step by step as per your plan. This is where your arithmetic skills and understanding of mathematical concepts are put to use.

- **Checking Your Work:** After arriving at a solution, it's crucial to check your work. This involves revising each step to ensure no errors were made, and confirming that the solution logically follows from the given information and adheres to any constraints of the problem.

- **Reflecting on the Process:** Finally, reflect on the solution process. Consider if there was a more efficient method or if you learned something new that could be applied to similar problems in the future.

Breaking Down Complex Problems

- **Identifying Sub-Problems:** Complex problems often consist of several smaller problems. Start by identifying these sub-problems. Breaking the problem into smaller, more manageable parts makes it less daunting and easier to approach.

- **Solving Each Part Individually:** Tackle each sub-problem one at a time, using the step-by-step approach. Solving smaller problems can provide insights or solutions that help in addressing the larger problem.

- **Integration for the Final Solution:** Once each sub-problem is solved, integrate these solutions to solve the larger problem. This step requires a synthesis of all the smaller solutions and understanding how they fit together.

- **Logical Progression:** Ensure that each step logically leads to the next. If you find that solving one part of the problem affects another part you've already solved, take a step back and reassess your approach.

- **Flexibility in Approach:** Be flexible in your approach. If you find that one method isn't working, don't hesitate to try a different strategy. Sometimes, stepping away and returning to a problem later can also provide new perspectives.

By mastering these problem-solving techniques, you will not only be able to tackle HSPT questions more effectively but also develop skills that are valuable in many real-world situations. Understanding and implementing these strategies will help you approach mathematical problems with confidence and precision.

Numerical Logic Puzzles

Numerical logic puzzles are an engaging way to develop and test your quantitative reasoning skills. These puzzles require more than just mathematical calculations; they challenge you to use logical thinking and deductive reasoning to arrive at a solution. Let's delve into understanding these puzzles and explore strategies for solving them.

Understanding Logic Puzzles

- What Are Numerical Logic Puzzles?: These puzzles involve numbers and sets of rules or conditions. The objective is often to fill in missing numbers or to determine the sequence or relationship between a given set of numbers. Unlike straightforward arithmetic problems, logic puzzles require you to figure out the 'how' and 'why' behind the correct answer.

- Types of Logic Puzzles: There are various types of numerical logic puzzles, including Sudoku, magic squares, nonograms, KenKen, and number sequence puzzles. Each type has its unique set of rules and challenges.

- Using Deductive Reasoning: Solving these puzzles often involves deductive reasoning, where you start with a set of possibilities and use the given information to reduce these possibilities to find the correct solution. It's about making logical deductions based on the provided clues.

Strategies for Solving

- Identifying Patterns: Many numerical logic puzzles are based on patterns. Look for recurring sequences, arithmetic operations, or relationships between numbers. Identifying the underlying pattern is often key to solving the puzzle.

- Process of Elimination: In puzzles where you have multiple possibilities, use the process of elimination. Discard options that don't fit the given conditions or rules. This narrows down the choices and makes it easier to find the solution.

- Working Backwards: Sometimes it's easier to start with the desired outcome and work backwards. Consider what conditions or sequences could lead to that outcome and see if they align with the given information.

- Breaking Down Complex Puzzles: For more complex puzzles, break them down into smaller sections or steps. Solve each section or step individually, then see how they fit together to solve the larger puzzle.

- Logical Guessing: At times, you might have to make an educated guess. Choose the option that seems most logical based on the information you have, then see if it leads to a valid solution. If it doesn't, backtrack and try a different option.

- Keeping Track of Your Reasoning: As you work through a puzzle, keep track of your reasoning and the conclusions you've reached. This not only helps in avoiding repeating the same steps but also aids in understanding where your reasoning might have gone wrong if you need to backtrack.

- Practicing Different Puzzle Types: Familiarize yourself with different types of numerical logic puzzles. Each type will challenge and develop different aspects of your logical and numerical reasoning.

Numerical logic puzzles are not only about testing your mathematical skills but also about sharpening your logical thinking and problem-solving abilities. They encourage you to look beyond the obvious and think critically about the information presented to you. By regularly practicing these puzzles and employing these strategies, you'll enhance your ability to tackle not just the puzzles themselves but any problem that requires logical and numerical reasoning.

Quantitative Comparison Strategies

Quantitative comparison questions, a common component in tests like the HSPT, require students to compare numerical values or mathematical expressions to determine which is greater, or whether they are equal. These questions test not only basic arithmetic skills but also the ability to critically analyze and estimate values. Let's explore the strategies for effectively comparing quantities and avoiding common traps in these types of questions.

Comparing Quantities

- Understanding the Question Format: Typically, quantitative comparison questions present two quantities, labeled Quantity A and Quantity B. You might be asked to determine if Quantity A is greater, Quantity B is greater, both are equal, or if there is not enough information to make a determination.

- Estimation Skills: Often, exact calculations aren't necessary; estimation can be sufficient to compare two quantities. For example, if Quantity A is slightly less than 1/2 and Quantity B is 1/3, you can estimate that Quantity A is greater without calculating the exact values.

- Breaking Down Complex Expressions: When dealing with algebraic or geometric expressions, break them down into simpler components. This simplification can make it easier to compare the quantities.

- Using Number Substitution: In algebraic comparisons, substituting numbers for variables can be a quick way to compare quantities. Choose simple numbers like 1, 0, or -1, and ensure they comply with any given conditions.

- Comparative Techniques: Develop an understanding of how to use inequalities, ratios, and proportions in comparison. This understanding is particularly useful in problems where you need to compare rates, percentages, or proportional relationships.

Avoiding Common Traps

- Overlooking Conditions or Restrictions: Always read the question carefully. Pay attention to any conditions or restrictions given for the quantities. Ignoring these can lead to incorrect conclusions.

- Avoiding Assumptions: Do not make assumptions beyond what is stated in the question. For instance, do not assume numbers are integers if not specified, or that figures are drawn to scale in geometry problems.

- Being Cautious with Extremes: Be wary of extreme values, especially when dealing with variables. What may be true for one set of numbers might not hold for another. For example, an inequality that holds for positive numbers may not hold for negative numbers.

- Recognizing Indeterminate Forms: Sometimes, it may not be possible to determine the relationship between two quantities with the information given. Recognize when this is the case, as one of the answer choices may be that the relationship cannot be determined.

- Double Checking Work: Always take a moment to review your comparisons. A common mistake is correctly computing or estimating the values but then incorrectly concluding which is greater or if they are equal.

By mastering these strategies and being aware of common pitfalls, you can approach quantitative comparison questions on the HSPT with confidence. This skill set not only aids in test-taking but also in making reasoned judgments based on numerical data in real-world situations. Remember, practice and familiarity with a wide range of problem types are key to becoming proficient in quantitative comparisons.

Exercises SET 1

Arithmetic Drills

1. Calculate the sum of 243 and 567.
2. Subtract 136 from 405.
3. Multiply 78 by 32.
4. Divide 1440 by 48.

Basic Algebra Problems

1. Solve for x: 3x + 5 = 20
2. If 2y - 4 = 10, find the value of y.
3. Simplify the expression: 4(3a + 5) - 2a
4. Solve for z: 2z/3 = 8

Logic Puzzles

1. If five cats catch five mice in five minutes, how many cats are needed to catch 100 mice in 100 minutes?
2. There are three light switches outside a room. One of the switches controls a light bulb inside the room. You can only enter the room once. How can you determine which switch controls the bulb?

Quantitative Comparison Questions

For these questions, determine whether:

- Quantity A is greater
- Quantity B is greater
- The two quantities are equal
- There is not enough information to determine the relationship

1. Quantity A: The product of 4 and 7

   Quantity B: The sum of 12 and 16

2. Quantity A: $\frac{1}{2}$ of 100

   Quantity B: 25% of 200

ANSWERS SET 1

Arithmetic Drills:

1. 810
2. 269
3. 2496
4. 30

Basic Algebra Problems:

1. x = 5
2. y = 7
3. 12a + 20 - 2a = 10a + 20
4. z = 12

Logic Puzzles:

1. Five cats. The number of cats is irrelevant to the time it takes to catch the mice.
2. Turn on the first switch and leave it on for a few minutes. Then, turn it off, turn on the second switch and enter the room. If the bulb is on, it's the second switch. If it's off but warm, it's the first switch. If it's off and cold, it's the third switch.

Quantitative Comparison Questions:

Quantity A is greater (28 > 28)

The two quantities are equal (50 = 50)

Exercises SET 2

Arithmetic Drills

- Find the product of 123 and 11.

- Divide 567 by 9 and find the quotient.

- Subtract 258 from 789.

- Add 432, 567, and 321 together.

Advanced Algebra Problems

1. Solve for x: $5x - 7 = 3x + 9$

2. If $4x + 5 = 21$, find the value of x.

3. Simplify the expression: $2(5b - 3) + 4b$

4. Solve for y: $y/3 - 2 = 4$

Additional Logic Puzzles

1. A grandfather, two fathers, and two sons went fishing. Each caught one fish. How many fish were caught in total?

2. You have two ropes. Each takes exactly 60 minutes to burn from one end to the other. The ropes are of different densities, so burning half of a rope does not necessarily take 30 minutes. How can you measure exactly 45 minutes?

More Quantitative Comparison Questions

1. Quantity A: The square of 9

   Quantity B: The square root of 81

2. Quantity A: Half of 150

   Quantity B: 30% of 500

ANSWERS SET 2

Arithmetic Drills

1. The product of 123 and 11 is 1353.

2. The quotient of 567 divided by 9 is 63.

3. When you subtract 258 from 789, the result is 531.

4. Adding 432, 567, and 321 together gives a sum of 1320.

Advanced Algebra Problems

1. For the equation $5x - 7 = 3x + 9$, the value of x is 8.

2. If $4x + 5 = 21$, then the value of x is 4.

3. Simplifying the expression $2(5b - 3) + 4b$ gives you $14b - 6$.

4. Solving $y/3 - 2 = 4$ gives you $y = 18$.

Additional Logic Puzzles

1. If a grandfather, two fathers, and two sons went fishing and each caught one fish, they caught a total of 3 fish because the grandfather is also a father, and the father is also a son.

2. To measure exactly 45 minutes using the two ropes: Start by lighting one rope at both ends and the other rope at one end. When the first rope has burned out completely (30 minutes), light the other end of the second rope. Since the second rope has been burning from one end for 30 minutes, it will take another 15 minutes to burn out completely once it's lit from both ends, totaling 45 minutes.

More Quantitative Comparison Questions

1. Quantity A (the square of 9, which is 81) is equal to Quantity B (the square root of 81, which is also 9).

2. Quantity A (half of 150, which is 75) is less than Quantity B (30% of 500, which is 150).

CHAPTER 4: READING WITH PURPOSE

Stepping into the world of reading comprehension, Chapter 4 of this guide is dedicated to equipping you with strategies to navigate through passages with an analytical eye, identify central themes, and develop strong inference skills that are essential for the HSPT.

Critical Analysis: Interpreting Text

Critical analysis in reading comprehension is a multifaceted process that involves delving into the text to understand the author's intentions, the message being conveyed, and the means by which the text communicates this message. This process requires a reader to be both reflective and evaluative while reading. Let's expand on the components of critical analysis:

- Determining the Author's Purpose: Authors write with different purposes: to inform, persuade, entertain, or express themselves. Identifying why the author wrote the passage provides a lens through which the content can be interpreted. For instance, persuasive texts may use emotional language to influence readers, while informative texts might prioritize clarity and factual information.

- Analyzing the Text Structure: The organization of a text contributes significantly to its meaning. For example, a narrative structure with a clear beginning, middle, and end can guide readers through a story, while a compare and contrast structure may be used to highlight differences or similarities between concepts. Understanding the structure helps in predicting and locating information.

- Evaluating Arguments and Evidence: When an author presents an argument, it is important to critically evaluate the strength and relevance of the evidence provided. This involves questioning the validity of the data, the reliability of sources, and the logic of the arguments made.

- Recognizing Bias and Assumptions: Texts often reflect the author's own perspectives or biases, whether intentional or not. Identifying these biases is crucial as they can shape the content and influence the reader's interpretation. Readers should be aware of loaded language, generalizations, and selective presentation of facts, all of which can indicate an author's bias.

- Interpreting Language and Tone: The choice of words (diction) and the attitude conveyed (tone) can offer insights into the text's deeper meanings. A text with a formal tone may convey seriousness, while a casual tone might be used for lighter topics or to connect with the reader on a personal level.

- Considering the Historical or Cultural Context: Understanding the time period or culture from which the text originates can provide important background that informs the text's themes and content. This context can affect everything from the themes and issues considered important to the language and references used.

- Drawing Inferences: Beyond what is explicitly stated, readers should draw inferences about what is implied by the text. This might involve predicting outcomes, discerning themes, and understanding character motivations in a story, or identifying the implications of an argument.

- Reflecting on Personal Response: A critical analysis also involves reflecting on one's own response to the text. Does it align with your experiences or challenge your beliefs? How does this personal engagement with the text shape your understanding of it?

Theme Identification: Uncovering the Core Message

Theme identification is a critical reading skill that involves discerning the central or underlying message the author wishes to convey through a passage. It goes beyond the surface details of the plot or subject matter to uncover the deeper significance of the text. Let's delve into the process and nuances of identifying a theme.

Understanding Theme in Literature

A theme is not just a topic, but an opinion or statement about life and human nature that the author expresses through the narrative. It's the lesson or moral that the reader is meant to learn or consider.

Identifying the Theme

- Recurring Subjects: One of the first steps in identifying the theme is to note the subjects that come up repeatedly throughout the text. For instance, if a passage frequently discusses wealth and poverty, the theme may revolve around the socio-economic disparities in society.

- Character Development: Observe the main characters' journeys and transformations. Themes often relate to what the characters learn or how they change. If a character moves from selfishness to generosity, the theme might relate to the value of altruism.

- Conflict: Conflict is a driving force in many narratives and often central to the theme. It can be external (character vs. character, society, nature) or internal (character vs. self). Identifying the main conflict can lead to understanding the theme, such as the struggle for self-identity or freedom.

- Narrative Voice and Tone: The way a story is told, and the tone the author uses, can also indicate the theme. A sarcastic tone might point towards a theme of disillusionment, while an earnest one could suggest hope or sincerity.

- Symbols and Imagery: Authors often use symbols and imagery to reinforce the theme. A recurring symbol like a bird in flight might represent freedom, while stormy weather could symbolize turmoil or conflict.

- Dialogue and Statements: Pay attention to what the characters say, especially any philosophical or reflective statements they make. These often reveal the author's message.

- Title and Headings: Sometimes, the title of the passage or headings within the text can give clues about the theme. They are often chosen carefully to reflect the central message.

Why Theme Identification Matters

Understanding the theme of a passage is vital for several reasons:

- Comprehension: It enhances overall comprehension of the text and allows for a deeper engagement with the material.

- Interpretation: It informs your interpretation of events, characters, and the author's purpose.

- Analysis: It is crucial for analysis, especially when answering essay questions or engaging in discussions about the text.

- Connection: Themes often reflect universal truths or experiences, allowing readers to connect the text to their own lives or to larger societal issues.

Identifying the theme is not always straightforward and can require thoughtful consideration and sometimes multiple readings of a text. It involves piecing together different elements of the narrative and interpreting them in a way that reveals a deeper understanding of the author's message. Through practice, readers become more adept at quickly pinpointing themes, which is a skill that can significantly benefit one's performance on the reading comprehension section of the HSPT.

Inference Skills: Reading Between the Lines

Inference skills are essential for deep reading comprehension and are particularly crucial when tackling standardized tests like the HSPT. To infer is to draw conclusions from information that is suggested but not overtly stated. This skill requires a reader to use both the explicit content of the text and their own reasoning to understand the underlying messages or themes.

Here's a deeper look at how to develop and apply inference skills:

Gathering Evidence

Inference begins with gathering evidence. This involves carefully reading the text and noting details that may seem minor but are actually significant. It could be a character's tone, a shift in the setting, or a particular choice of words. These details are the pieces of evidence that will support your inferential conclusions.

Understanding Context

Context is key to making accurate inferences. It includes not only the immediate context of a sentence or paragraph but also the larger context of the entire passage. Historical context, cultural nuances, and genre conventions can all inform the meaning behind the text.

Analyzing Textual Clues

Authors often leave clues that point toward larger truths. These can be patterns of imagery, recurrent themes, or character behavior that hint at deeper issues. For example, if a character repeatedly looks out the window as they speak about their future, an inference might be that they are longing for change or freedom.

Employing Background Knowledge

Your own knowledge and experiences play a role in making inferences. Readers bring their understanding of the world to the text, which helps them make connections that aren't explicitly drawn by the author. This background knowledge can fill in the gaps where information is missing.

Asking Questions

Inferential readers are inquisitive. They ask questions about the text: Why would the character act this way? What does this description suggest about the setting? What can be understood from the relationship between characters? Asking such questions can guide you to inferential answers.

Making Predictions

Inferences often involve making predictions about what will happen next in a text based on the information given. Predictions are informed guesses that go beyond the evidence but are still rooted in the text.

Checking Inferences Against the Text

It's important to continually check your inferences against the text to ensure they are reasonable. If new information is presented that contradicts your inference, you may need to adjust your conclusions.

Practicing Inference Skills

To practice inference skills, you might:

- Read a passage and then explain the mood or tone, using specific references to the text for support.
- Describe the personality of a character without referring to direct descriptions, instead using the character's actions or dialogue as evidence.
- Read a poem and infer the broader theme or message, identifying the figurative language that guides your interpretation.

Inference is not about making wild guesses; it's about making thoughtful, educated conclusions based on the evidence presented. When reading, it's the inferential thinking that often leads to a richer understanding of the text, allowing you to grasp not just what is said, but what is meant. This skill is invaluable for success in the reading comprehension section of the HSPT, as it allows you to derive meanings that are implied rather than directly presented.

Efficient Reading: Maximizing Time and Comprehension

Efficient reading is a skill that balances speed with comprehension, particularly important in a timed test like the HSPT. The goal is to extract as much information as needed from a passage to answer questions correctly without wasting time on unnecessary details. Here's a closer look at how to develop this skill:

Focusing on Key Sentences

- Topic Sentences: In most well-structured paragraphs, the first sentence, known as the topic sentence, often provides the main idea. By focusing on these sentences, you can understand the overarching point without reading every detail that follows.

- Concluding Sentences: Similarly, the last sentence of a paragraph can sometimes summarize or conclude the main idea, reinforcing what's been said or suggesting the implications.

Summarizing Passages

- Mental Summaries: As you read, try to mentally summarize each paragraph in a few words. This keeps you actively engaged with the material and helps to reinforce the main points.

- Written Summaries: If allowed, jot down these summaries in the margin or on a piece of scratch paper. This will serve as a quick reference when answering questions.

Skimming for Main Ideas

- Skimming Techniques: Learn to let your eyes 'skim' over the text to spot key words or phrases. Skimming involves reading quickly to get a general idea of the content without focusing on every word.

- Structural Cues: Pay attention to headings, bolded words, lists, and other structural elements that can guide you to important information.

Navigating Details

- Selective Reading: Not all information in a passage is relevant to the questions you'll need to answer. Learn to identify and focus on the details that are likely to be important while skimming over less relevant content.

- Data and Examples: Watch for data, examples, or quotations that are often used to support the main ideas. Recognizing these can often help answer specific questions about the passage.

Improving Reading Speed

- Practice: The more you read, the faster and more efficient you become. Regular reading practice, especially with a variety of texts, can increase your reading speed and comprehension.

- Timed Practices: Regularly practicing with a timer can help you get a feel for the pace you need to maintain during the test.

Retention and Recall

- Active Engagement: Engage with the text by asking questions or predicting what might come next. This active engagement can help you retain information.

- Recall After Reading: After reading a passage, practice recalling the main points without looking back at the text. This exercise can improve your memory retention.

By honing these techniques, you can develop the ability to read efficiently—gathering necessary information quickly and effectively, which is essential for performing well on the reading comprehension section of the HSPT. Remember, efficient reading isn't about rushing through a passage but about reading in a smart, strategic way that maximizes both your time and your understanding of the material.

Annotating Text: An Active Reading Strategy

Annotation is a dynamic and interactive approach to reading comprehension that involves engaging with the text through thoughtful notes and marks. It's a strategy that encourages active reading, which is crucial for deep understanding and retention of material. Let's unpack this strategy in more detail:

- Why Annotate?: The main goal of annotating is to promote active thinking and foster a deeper connection with the material. When you annotate, you're less likely to passively skim over the text and more likely to consider its implications, arguments, and nuances.

- Underlining and Highlighting: Start by identifying and underlining or highlighting key phrases or terms that seem to be central to the passage's main idea or theme. This could include technical terms, names, dates, or any concept that stands out as significant.

- Making Marginal Notes: In the margins of the text (or on a separate note if the text can't be marked), jot down quick summaries of what you've read. This could be a brief restatement of a paragraph's main idea, an observation about the author's argument, or questions that occur to you as you read.

- Symbols and Codes: Develop a system of symbols and codes that can quickly denote your thoughts. For example, a question mark could indicate an area you don't understand, or an exclamation mark might denote surprise or a significant point. This shorthand can make the process of reviewing your annotations more efficient.

- Dialogue with the Text: Think of annotation as a conversation with the author. You can agree, disagree, or question the author's points. This dialogue helps to critically evaluate the text and form your own opinions.

- Marking Confusions and Questions: Whenever you encounter a statement or concept that is confusing, mark it. Write down your questions or what you think the text might mean. This not only keeps track of areas you need to explore further but also encourages you to engage deeply with the material.

- Summarizing Sections: After reading a section, write a summary in your own words. This reinforces what you've read and aids in consolidating your understanding of the text.

- Connecting Ideas: Use arrows or lines to connect ideas within the text that relate to each other. This can help in understanding the structure of the argument or narrative and in seeing the larger picture.

- Reviewing Annotations: Once you've finished reading and annotating, go back and review your marks. This review process can offer new insights and reinforce your understanding of the text.

By incorporating these detailed annotation strategies into your reading practice, you'll transform the way you interact with text, leading to a more fulfilling and productive reading experience.

Answering Questions with Precision

Answering questions with precision on reading comprehension sections like those on the HSPT involves a series of focused strategies that ensure your responses are accurate and supported by the text. Here is a detailed look at how to enhance precision in answering such questions:

Referencing Annotations

- Utilize Your Annotations: Your annotations serve as a map of the passage, highlighting the most important points, transitions, key vocabulary, and any queries you had while reading. When answering questions, these annotations will direct you to the relevant parts of the text quickly, allowing you to cross-reference the question with the passage.

- Evidence-Based Answers: For each question, look for annotations that pertain directly to the query. If a question asks about the author's argument, find the section of your annotations where you noted the main argument or thesis. Your answer should be supported by the text, not by assumptions or external knowledge.

Rereading When Necessary

- Targeted Rereading: If the question refers to a specific line or paragraph, go back and read that section carefully, even if you have already annotated it. This second look will help to confirm your understanding and might reveal nuances that were not immediately apparent during the initial reading.

- Contextual Clues: Sometimes the answer to a question isn't found in a single line but rather in the context around it. Pay attention to what comes before and after the referenced section to fully understand the implications.

Answer Choices Analysis

- Process of Elimination: Read all answer choices carefully. Eliminate choices that are clearly incorrect, that go beyond the text, or that distort the meaning of the passage. This narrows down the options and increases the likelihood of selecting the correct answer.

- Look for Direct Evidence: The best answer choice is the one that you can directly support with evidence from the passage. It should align with the information that the author provides and should be verifiable with a specific reference to the text.

- Beware of Traps: Common traps in answer choices include extremes (words like "always," "never," "the only"), distortions of the passage content, or choices that seem plausible but are not mentioned or supported by the text.

Critical Thinking

- Inference vs. Explicit Information: Determine whether the question requires an inference or if it is asking for explicitly stated information. For inference questions, ensure your conclusion is a reasonable deduction based on the text.

- Author's Purpose and Tone: Some questions may ask about the author's purpose or tone. Use your annotations to recall the overall mood of the passage and the author's intent, and select the answer that best reflects these.

- Question Wording: Pay close attention to the wording of the questions. The test-makers craft questions carefully, and understanding exactly what is being asked is crucial to selecting the correct answer.

By answering questions with precision, you are applying a critical eye to both the passage and the questions themselves. This methodical approach ensures that your answers are not only accurate but also demonstrably correct based on the text provided. The skills of annotation, targeted rereading, and critical analysis are your tools for achieving this level of precision in the reading comprehension section of the HSPT.

Practice Exercises

Passage 1: Literary Fiction

In a small village where the land met the sea, a young girl named Elara spent her days wandering the shore, collecting shells and listening to the tales of the old fishermen. They spoke of a time when the sea was full of life and the fish were plentiful. Now, the nets came back empty more often than not. The village had fallen on hard times, and many had left seeking better fortunes elsewhere. Yet, Elara remained, steadfast in her belief that the sea would provide once again.

Questions:

What is the main theme of the passage?

A) Adventure and exploration

B) Hardship and hope

C) Greed and prosperity

D) Isolation and abandonment

Based on the passage, what can be inferred about Elara's character?

A) She is naive and unworldly.

B) She is adventurous and curious.

C) She is optimistic and loyal.

D) She is melancholic and isolated.

Why do the nets come back empty?

A) The villagers don't fish properly.

B) There is a suggestion of environmental change.

C) The fishermen tell false tales.

D) Elara has scared the fish away.

Passage 2: Science Article

The Mimosa pudica plant, commonly known as the "sensitive plant", is famous for its rapid plant movement. When touched, the leaves fold inward and droop, a mechanism believed to deter predators. This fascinating response is a survival adaptation that has intrigued scientists for centuries. Recent studies suggest that this movement triggers a water release from the leaf cells, altering turgor pressure and causing the leaves to close.

Questions:

What is the primary purpose of the Mimosa pudica's leaf movement?

A) To entertain humans

B) To conserve water

C) To protect itself from harm

D) To attract insects

What causes the Mimosa pudica's leaves to close?

A) A chemical reaction in the air

B) A change in turgor pressure in the leaf cells

C) The onset of nighttime

D) Dehydration of the plant

Passage 3: Historical Excerpt

The Industrial Revolution marked a major turning point in history; almost every aspect of daily life was influenced in some way. Arguably, the most significant changes took place in the economic field. Mechanization led to the creation of new industries and the development of new forms of labor organization. The factory system replaced the cottage industry, and masses of workers found themselves in urban centers.

Questions:

What was one significant effect of the Industrial Revolution?

A) The decline of urban centers

B) The expansion of the cottage industry

C) The migration of workers to cities

D) The decrease in new industry creation

According to the excerpt, what was a major change during the Industrial Revolution?

A) The end of economic growth

B) The mechanization of labor

C) The decrease in labor needs

D) The stagnation of industrial development

When working through these exercises, remember to time yourself to simulate the conditions of the actual HSPT. After completing the questions, check your answers and reflect on your reasoning to ensure you understand each concept fully.

ANSWERS

Answers to Passage 1: Literary Fiction

The main theme of the passage is:

B) Hardship and hope

Based on the passage, what can be inferred about Elara's character is:

C) She is optimistic and loyal.

The nets come back empty because:

B) There is a suggestion of environmental change.

Answers to Passage 2: Science Article

The primary purpose of the Mimosa pudica's leaf movement is:

C) To protect itself from harm.

The Mimosa pudica's leaves close due to:

B) A change in turgor pressure in the leaf cells.

Answers to Passage 3: Historical Excerpt

One significant effect of the Industrial Revolution was:

C) The migration of workers to cities.

According to the excerpt, a major change during the Industrial Revolution was:

B) The mechanization of labor.

These answers are based on information directly from the passages or inferred from the context provided. Reviewing the reasoning behind each correct answer is as important as the practice itself, so be sure to understand why each answer is correct to improve your skills in reading comprehension.

CHAPTER 5: DEMYSTIFYING MATHEMATICS

Embarking on the journey through mathematics, this chapter serves as your compass to navigate the vast landscape of numbers, shapes, and data. Here, we will unravel the complexity of mathematical concepts and transform them into understandable and solvable problems.

Fundamental Concepts: The Building Blocks

In the realm of mathematics, the fundamental concepts act as the essential elements that form the basis of all further learning in the subject. These basics are akin to the alphabet and grammar of a language—a means to communicate and understand the more complex ideas that will follow.

Arithmetic Fundamentals

- Core Operations: These are the primary actions we can perform with numbers. Addition combines quantities, subtraction finds the difference between them, multiplication scales a number by another, and division apportion a quantity into equal parts. Each operation follows specific rules and has particular properties that govern how they are used.

- Efficient Methods: Efficiency in arithmetic means finding the quickest and most accurate route to the answer. This might involve recognizing patterns—for instance, understanding that multiplying by 10 simply adds a zero to the end of a number or that subtracting a number is the same as adding its negative.

- Mental Math Shortcuts: These are tricks and techniques used to perform calculations in your head. Examples include using rounding to estimate answers or breaking down complex calculations into simpler, more manageable ones (like splitting a multiplication problem into smaller, easier-to-multiply parts).

Algebraic Thinking

- Manipulating Expressions: Algebra introduces symbols, often letters, to represent numbers. Learning algebra involves understanding how to manipulate these symbols according to the rules of arithmetic to simplify expressions or solve equations.

- Solving Equations: An equation is a statement that two expressions are equal. Solving an equation means finding the value of the variable that makes the equation true. This often involves a series of steps that reverse the operations applied to the variable.
- Functions and Formulas: Functions are special types of equations that describe a relationship between quantities. Understanding a function means being able to determine the output for a given input, according to the rule specified by the function.

Properties of Numbers

- Commutative Law: This property states that the order in which you add or multiply numbers does not affect the result. For example, 3 + 4 is the same as 4 + 3, and the same goes for multiplication.
- Associative Law: This law states that when adding or multiplying several numbers, the way in which they are grouped does not affect the outcome. For example, (2 + 3) + 4 is the same as 2 + (3 + 4).
- Distributive Law: This property is a strategy for multiplying a number by a sum or difference. It allows for the number to be distributed across the addition or subtraction within the brackets, simplifying complex expressions. For example, 2*(3 + 4) is the same as (23) + (24).

Advanced Topics: Expanding Your Horizons

Mathematics is a dynamic field that extends into dimensions both seen and unseen. As foundational skills are mastered, the subject beckons students into more advanced territories that challenge the intellect and spark the imagination.

Geometry in Space

- Understanding Spatial Relationships: When studying geometry, it's essential to understand how shapes relate to each other in space. This includes comprehending concepts such as parallelism, perpendicularity, and symmetry.
- Properties of Shapes: Delve into the attributes of different shapes—triangles, quadrilaterals, circles, and polygons. Explore how their angles, sides, and other features define them and set the stage for more complex geometric reasoning.

- Theorems and Proofs: Geometry is rich with theorems that explain the relationships between different parts of shapes. For instance, the Pythagorean theorem connects the sides of right-angled triangles in a way that is both beautiful and practical. Understanding these theorems often involves following or constructing a proof—a logical argument that establishes the truth of the theorem.

- Area and Volume Calculation: Move from calculating the area of two-dimensional shapes to finding the volume of three-dimensional objects. This transition requires visualizing how shapes extend into space and using formulas that account for their depth.

- Geometric Representation: Practice skills in geometric drawing and reading. Accurately drawing shapes and reading geometric diagrams are crucial for understanding complex problems, especially when it comes to interpreting real-world scenarios.

The Dance of Statistics

- Graphical Interpretation: Statistics often utilize graphs to present data in a digestible form. Learn to interpret various types of graphs, such as bar graphs, line graphs, pie charts, and histograms, understanding what each type reveals about the underlying data.

- Measures of Central Tendency: Central tendency measures—mean, median, and mode—offer a way to summarize data with a single value that represents the center of the data's distribution. Each measure gives different insights, and knowing when to use each one is key.

- Dispersion and Range: Beyond central tendencies, understand how spread out data is with concepts like range, variance, and standard deviation. These measures help in understanding the variability in data sets.

- Probability Fundamentals: Probability is the mathematics of chance and uncertainty. Grasp the basics of probability, learning how to calculate the likelihood of events based on possible outcomes and understanding the fundamental principles like independent and dependent events.

- Predictive Statistics: Use probability to make predictions. This involves understanding how to model different scenarios and calculate the expected outcomes of random events, which is essential not just for academic exercises but also for real-world decision-making.

As you expand your horizons into these advanced topics, you're not just learning mathematics; you're learning new ways to interpret the world. Geometry helps you understand the space around you, while statistics provide the tools to make sense of the vast amounts of information you encounter in daily life. Both disciplines foster critical thinking and analytical skills that are valuable in a wide range of academic and professional fields.

Mathematical Reasoning: The Why Behind the What

Understanding mathematical reasoning involves delving into the rationale and logic that underpin mathematical concepts and formulas, moving beyond memorizing rules to comprehending their essence. This deeper insight is crucial for true mastery of mathematics.

1. Understanding the Foundations:

- Beyond Memorization: The goal is to understand the principles behind mathematical formulas and operations. For instance, why does the Pythagorean theorem work, or what is the logic behind the formula for the area of a circle? This understanding leads to a more profound and intuitive grasp of mathematics.

- Interconnections: Mathematics is a web of interconnected concepts. Understanding how different areas of mathematics relate to each other, such as how algebra underpins calculus, enriches the learning experience and enhances problem-solving skills.

Logical Flow: Constructing and Deconstructing Arguments

1. Logical Progression in Mathematics:

- Building Arguments: Mathematical proofs and solutions are built through a logical progression of steps. Each step follows from the previous one based on established mathematical principles, forming a chain of reasoning that leads to the conclusion.

- Critical Analysis: Learning to construct mathematical proofs involves understanding how to start from known information and logically arrive at a new conclusion. Conversely, deconstructing proofs involves analyzing each step to understand how it contributes to the overall argument.

2. Application in Problem Solving:

- Systematic Approach: When solving problems, a systematic approach based on logical flow is crucial. This involves identifying given information, determining what is to be proven or found, and then methodically applying mathematical principles to reach a solution.
- Validating Solutions: The logical flow also involves critically assessing the solution to ensure that it is valid and that each step logically follows from the last.

Problem Types: Strategy and Approach

1. Classifying Problems:

- Diverse Types: Problems in mathematics can range from straightforward computational tasks to complex, multi-step problems. Recognizing the type of problem at hand is the first step in determining the appropriate approach.
- Classification Criteria: Problems can be classified based on various criteria, such as the mathematical concept involved (e.g., geometry, algebra), the skills required (e.g., calculation, logical reasoning), or the form of the problem (e.g., word problem, proof).

2. Matching Problems with Strategies:

- Direct Calculation: Some problems require direct application of formulas or arithmetic operations. These are usually straightforward but require accuracy in calculation.
- Pattern Recognition: Other problems, especially in areas like algebra or number theory, may involve recognizing patterns or sequences. Identifying these patterns can often lead to quicker and more elegant solutions.

- Problem-Solving Heuristics: For more complex problems, employing problem-solving heuristics (like working backwards, making a drawing, or considering special cases) can be effective. These strategies help break down the problem and make it more manageable.

- Adaptive Thinking: Often, a combination of strategies is needed. Being able to adaptively think and switch strategies as needed is a critical skill in mathematical problem-solving.

In summary, mathematical reasoning is about understanding the 'why' behind the 'what.' It's about building a logical foundation for mathematical arguments, learning to analyze and construct proofs and solutions, and developing versatile problem-solving skills that can be adapted to a wide range of problem types. This comprehensive approach to mathematics not only prepares students for academic challenges but also fosters a deeper appreciation of the beauty and logic inherent in mathematical thought.

Applying Concepts: Real-World Scenarios

Mathematics is an essential tool for interpreting and navigating the complexities of the world around us. It provides a framework for understanding patterns, solving problems, and making informed decisions. In this section, we focus on two key aspects of applying mathematical concepts to real-world scenarios: tackling application problems and engaging in critical thinking challenges.

Application Problems: Bridging Theory and Practice

- Translating Words into Numbers: Real-world problems are often presented in words, and a major skill in mathematics is translating these words into mathematical expressions. This involves identifying key pieces of information, determining which mathematical operations to use, and constructing an equation or set of equations that models the situation.

- Extracting Relevant Information: Many word problems include information that is not necessary for solving the problem. Learning to distinguish between relevant and irrelevant information is crucial. This skill involves honing in on the numbers and relationships that will directly contribute to finding the solution.

- Building Models: Real-world scenarios can often be modeled using geometric shapes, algebraic expressions, or statistical data. For instance, predicting the cost of a project might involve linear equations, while planning a garden might require area and perimeter calculations.

- Iterative Approach: Sometimes the first model you create isn't quite right. Applying mathematical concepts often requires an iterative approach, where you refine your model based on new information or a deeper understanding of the problem.

Critical Thinking Challenges: Applying Mathematics Creatively

- Puzzles and Non-Routine Problems: These challenges push you to apply mathematical concepts in new and unexpected ways. They require a deep understanding of mathematical principles and the creativity to use them in non-standard situations.

- Strategic Problem Solving: Unlike routine problems, puzzles and non-routine problems may not have a clear path to the solution. You must decide which mathematical tools to use and how to apply them, often trying multiple strategies before finding one that works.

- Developing Reasoning Skills: These problems enhance your reasoning skills by forcing you to explain why a particular solution works. They often have multiple valid approaches, and part of the challenge is justifying your chosen method.

- Connecting Different Areas of Mathematics: A single puzzle may involve geometry, algebra, and number theory. Recognizing how different areas of mathematics can inform each other is a valuable skill in solving complex problems.

Through the process of tackling application problems and engaging with critical thinking challenges, you not only practice the mathematics you've learned but also develop a versatile skill set. This set can be applied to a wide range of situations—from everyday decisions to complex professional tasks. It empowers you to view mathematics not as a series of abstract concepts but as a practical and powerful tool for interpreting and influencing the world around you.

Practice Exercises

1. Logical Reasoning:

Given: All circles are shapes. All shapes have area. Does it logically follow that all circles have area?

Provide a logical justification for your answer.

2. Algebraic Proof:

Prove that if a+b=c, then 4a+4b=4c.

3. Geometry Problem-Solving:

A rectangle has a length that is twice its width. If the perimeter of the rectangle is 36 cm, find its area.

4. Number Theory:

Show that the sum of any two even numbers is always even.

5. Pattern Recognition:

What is the next number in the sequence: 2, 4, 8, 16, ...?

6. Word Problem:

A train travels 60 miles in 1.5 hours. At the same speed, how far will it travel in 3 hours?

7. Problem-Solving Heuristics:

There are 23 apples in a basket. If you remove 3 apples and replace them with 1 orange, how many fruits will be in the basket after repeating this process 5 times?

8. Logical Flow in Algebra:

Solve for x:

2(x−3)+4=x+6.

Explain each step of your solution.

9. Statistical Reasoning:

A student scores 85, 90, 75, and 80 on four tests. What score must they achieve on the fifth test to have an average of 80?

10. Geometry Proof:

Prove that the angles in a triangle always sum up to 180 degrees.

ANSWERS

1. Yes, it logically follows since all circles are shapes and all shapes have area.

2. By the distributive property, $4a+4b=4(c)$.

3. Area = 48 cm² (Width = 6 cm, Length = 12 cm).

4. Even + Even = Even (e.g., 2 + 4 = 6).

5. 32 (Each number is double the previous one).

6. 120 miles (Speed = 40 mph).

7. 18 fruits (15 apples, 3 oranges).

8. $x=10$ (Distribute, then solve the linear equation).

9. Score 80 (Average formula: Total/5 = 80).

10. Angle sum property (Various proofs possible, like using parallel lines and alternate interior angles).

CHAPTER 6: LANGUAGE SKILLS FOR SUCCESS

This chapter is your roadmap to mastering the language skills essential for the HSPT. Here, we focus on the intricacies of English grammar, punctuation, and effective sentence construction. Our goal is to enhance your writing clarity and coherence, ensuring you are well-prepared for the language section of the HSPT.

Understanding Grammar: The Backbone of Language

Grammar, as the set of rules that govern the use of words in a language, forms the backbone of effective communication. A solid understanding of grammar is crucial for constructing clear, precise, and meaningful sentences. Let's explore its key components in detail:

1. Parts of Speech: Foundations of Sentence Construction

- Nouns: These are words that name people, places, things, or ideas. Understanding nouns is essential as they often serve as the subject of a sentence.

- Verbs: Verbs express actions or states of being. They are central to sentences, as they indicate what the subject is doing or experiencing.

- Adjectives: These describe or modify nouns, providing more detail about them, such as size, color, or quantity.

- Adverbs: Adverbs modify verbs, adjectives, or other adverbs, often indicating manner, place, time, or degree.

- Pronouns: Pronouns replace nouns to avoid repetition. They must agree in number and gender with the nouns they replace.

- Prepositions: Prepositions show relationships between a noun or pronoun and other words in a sentence, usually indicating direction, place, time, or method.

- Conjunctions: These join words, phrases, or clauses together, helping to build complex thoughts.

- Interjections: Interjections are words or phrases that express strong emotion or surprise and are usually set apart from the rest of the sentence by an exclamation point or a comma.

2. Sentence Structure: Crafting Varied and Engaging Sentences

- Simple Sentences: Consist of one independent clause that has a subject and a verb and expresses a complete thought.
- Compound Sentences: Formed by joining two independent clauses with a conjunction, a semicolon, or a comma.
- Complex Sentences: Contain one independent clause and at least one dependent clause, which cannot stand alone as a sentence.
- Compound-Complex Sentences: Combine elements of compound and complex sentences, featuring at least two independent clauses and one or more dependent clauses.

Varying sentence structure in your writing keeps it engaging and dynamic, preventing it from becoming monotonous.

3. Subject-Verb Agreement: Ensuring Grammatical Harmony

- The verb in a sentence must agree with its subject in number (singular or plural) and person. This rule remains one of the foundations of grammatical correctness.
- Common issues include dealing with compound subjects, collective nouns, and indefinite pronouns, each requiring specific agreement rules.

4. Tenses and Mood: Conveying Time and Attitude

- Tenses: Understanding verb tenses (past, present, future, and their variations) is crucial for indicating when an action or state of being occurs. Mastery of tenses ensures clarity and precision in describing events.
- Mood: This aspect of verbs indicates the speaker's attitude toward the action/state of the verb, whether it's a fact (indicative mood), a command (imperative mood), a wish/doubt (subjunctive mood), or a condition contrary to fact.

Mastering Punctuation: The Art of Clarity

Punctuation marks play an essential role in writing, serving as tools to clarify the meaning of sentences and to guide readers through the text. They function much like road signs, signaling stops, pauses, connections, and other navigational aids in the flow of ideas.

1. Commas, Periods, and Semicolons: Essential Tools for Clarity

- Commas (,): The comma is one of the most versatile punctuation marks. It's used to separate items in a list, set off introductory elements, and create a pause in a sentence, giving the reader a brief break. Commas also separate clauses and phrases within sentences to prevent misreading. For example, in a complex sentence, commas can clarify which clauses are dependent and which are independent.

- Periods (.): The period signifies a full stop at the end of a sentence. It indicates that one complete thought has ended and another is about to begin. Periods are crucial for maintaining clarity and preventing run-on sentences, which can confuse readers.

- Semicolons (;): Semicolons are often underutilized but are incredibly useful. They link closely related independent clauses. A semicolon can replace a period if the writer wishes to narrow the gap between two closely linked sentences. For example, instead of two separate sentences, a semicolon can link clauses in a compound sentence where the clauses are not joined by a conjunction.

2. Colons and Dashes: Adding Information and Emphasis

- Colons (:): Colons act as a gateway, signaling that what follows is an explanation or elaboration of what precedes. They are commonly used before lists, quotes, and sometimes before an explanation that is preceded by a clause that could stand as a complete sentence. A colon can create anticipation, signaling that important information or a summary is coming up.

- Dashes (–, —): Dashes come in two types: en dash (–) and em dash (—). The em dash is longer and used more in sentences. It's used to create emphasis or to insert additional information into a sentence. Dashes can replace commas, parentheses, or colons, and are particularly useful when you want to create a dramatic pause or draw attention to certain information.

3. Apostrophes and Quotation Marks: Indicating Possession and Speech

- Apostrophes ('): Apostrophes have two primary uses: showing possession and indicating contractions. In possession, an apostrophe signifies ownership, as in "Mary's book." In contractions, apostrophes represent omitted letters, such as in "don't" for "do not."

- Quotation Marks (" "): Quotation marks are used to denote direct speech, quotes from other sources, or to highlight titles of short works like articles or poems. They are essential for indicating when words are taken from other sources or when the language is used in an unusual or ironic way.

Writing Skills: Crafting Coherent Text

Writing skills are essential not just for standardized tests like the HSPT, but they are also crucial for academic and professional success. The ability to express ideas clearly and coherently in writing is a valuable skill. Let's break down the components of this skill set:

1. Developing a Thesis

A thesis statement is the cornerstone of any effective essay. It serves as a guide for both the writer and the reader, indicating the central point or argument that the essay will discuss.

- Clarity and Conciseness: A good thesis statement is clear and concise. It should directly state the main argument or point in a way that leaves no doubt about the essay's purpose.

- Positioning: Typically, a thesis statement is placed at the end of the introductory paragraph. It sets the tone for the essay and provides a roadmap for what is to come.

- Argument Development: The thesis should be something that you can argue or provide evidence for. It shouldn't be a simple statement of fact, but rather something that requires explanation and support.
- Specificity: Avoid vague language in your thesis. Be specific about what you plan to discuss or analyze in your essay.

2. Organizing Ideas

The organization of ideas in an essay is critical for clarity and coherence. An essay should be structured in a way that each part contributes logically to the overall argument.

- Paragraph Structure: Each paragraph should deal with a single idea or aspect of the main topic. Start with a topic sentence that outlines the main idea of the paragraph.
- Supporting Sentences: After the topic sentence, include supporting sentences that provide evidence, examples, or explanations to back up the main idea of the paragraph.
- Logical Flow: The paragraphs should be arranged in a logical order, each flowing smoothly to the next. The order should support the development of your argument as stated in your thesis.
- Conclusion: Your essay should conclude with a paragraph that summarizes the main points and reiterates the thesis, ideally in a way that shows its broader implications or significance.

3. Transitional Phrases

Transitional phrases help to link ideas in your writing and guide the reader from one idea to the next. They are the glue that holds the parts of your argument together.

- Purpose of Transitions: Transitions can show the reader where one paragraph ends and another begins, provide contrast, illustrate similarities, or offer conclusions.
- Examples: Common transitional phrases include "furthermore," "however," "for example," "in conclusion," and "as a result."

- Placement: Transitional phrases can be placed at the beginning of a new paragraph to introduce a new idea or within a paragraph to link ideas together.

Variety: Use a variety of transitional phrases to avoid repetition and make your writing more interesting.

Practice Exercises

GRAMMAR EXERCISES

Identifying Parts of Speech:

1.In the sentence, "The swiftly flowing river was breathtaking," identify the parts of speech for each word.

Correcting Subject-Verb Agreement Errors:

2.Correct the error in this sentence: "The list of items are on the desk."

Verb Tense Exercises:

3.Rewrite the sentence in past tense: "They are walking to the new café near the park."

PUNCTUATION DRILLS

Comma Usage:

4.Insert commas where necessary: "In the dark of night a mysterious figure appeared."

Semicolon and Colon Usage:

5.Use a semicolon or a colon correctly in this sentence: "I have two favorite foods pizza and pasta."

Apostrophe for Possession:

6.Correct the apostrophe usage in this sentence: "The cat's whiskers were unusually long for a kitten."

WRITING TASKS

Short Essay Writing – Thesis Development:

7.Write a thesis statement for an essay on the topic: "The impact of technology on education."

Paragraph Structure:

8.Write a paragraph discussing one major benefit of reading books. Include a topic sentence, supporting sentences, and a concluding sentence.

Using Transitions:

9.Write two separate sentences about environmental conservation. Then, combine them into one smooth sentence using a transitional phrase.

ANSWERS

Grammar Exercises

1. The (determiner), swiftly (adverb), flowing (adjective), river (noun), was (verb), breathtaking (adjective).

2. Corrected sentence: "The list of items is on the desk."

3. Past tense: "They walked to the new café near the park."

Punctuation Drills

4. With commas: "In the dark of night, a mysterious figure appeared."

5. With semicolon/colon: "I have two favorite foods: pizza and pasta."

6. Correct apostrophe usage: "The cats' whiskers were unusually long for kittens."

Writing Tasks

7. Thesis Statement: "The advent of technology has profoundly transformed educational landscapes, enhancing access to information and fostering innovative teaching methodologies."

8. Paragraph example: "Reading books extensively broadens our horizons. It exposes us to new ideas, cultures, and philosophies, thereby enhancing our knowledge and empathy. Books also improve our cognitive abilities, including memory and concentration. Thus, reading not only entertains but also enriches our minds."

9. Transition example: "Environmental conservation is crucial for sustaining biodiversity. Additionally, it is essential for maintaining a balanced ecosystem."

CHAPTER 7: THE PSYCHOLOGY OF TEST-TAKING

This chapter is dedicated to understanding and mastering the psychological aspects of test-taking. Navigating the mental challenges of an important exam like the HSPT is as vital as mastering the academic content. Here, we offer strategies to overcome test anxiety, maintain a positive mindset, and stay calm and focused both during your preparation and on the actual exam day.

Understanding Test Anxiety

Test anxiety is a type of performance anxiety that can affect anyone from primary school students to adults taking professional certifications. It's a psychological condition where individuals experience extreme distress and anxiety in testing situations, which can significantly impact their performance. Let's delve into various aspects of understanding test anxiety:

1. Symptoms of Test Anxiety

- Physical Symptoms: These can include sweating, shaking, rapid heartbeat, dry mouth, nausea, and headaches. Physically, the body may react as if it's in a high-stress situation, triggering a 'fight or flight' response.

- Emotional Symptoms: Feelings of fear, disappointment, anger, or helplessness. There can be a fear of failure, negative self-talk, and sometimes an irrational belief that one's self-worth is tied to the test performance.

- Cognitive Symptoms: Difficulty concentrating, blanking out, and racing thoughts are common. In some cases, students may experience negative thoughts about their capabilities and the consequences of failing.

2. Causes of Test Anxiety

- Fear of Failure: Often rooted in high expectations from oneself or others, fear of failure is a primary cause. This fear can be exacerbated in high-stakes testing environments.

- Lack of Preparation: Feeling unprepared can heighten anxiety. This may be due to inadequate study time, poor study habits, or previous poor performance in similar situations.

- High Pressure: In today's competitive academic environments, there's significant pressure to perform well, which can intensify test anxiety.

- Previous Negative Experiences: Past experiences with tests, especially if they were negative or traumatic, can contribute to developing test anxiety in future situations.

3. Impact of Test Anxiety

- Performance: High anxiety levels can impair memory and concentration, leading to difficulties in recalling information and focusing on the test.

- Physical and Emotional Health: Prolonged anxiety can have long-term effects on physical and emotional health, leading to issues like chronic stress, depression, or anxiety disorders.

- Academic Consequences: Test anxiety can result in lower test scores, which can affect academic progression and opportunities.

4. Managing Test Anxiety

- Recognition and Acceptance: The first step in managing test anxiety is recognizing its presence and understanding that it's a common experience for many people.

- Preparation and Study Skills: Adequate preparation and effective study habits can significantly reduce anxiety. This includes creating a study plan, using active learning techniques, and practicing under test-like conditions.

- Mindfulness and Relaxation Techniques: Practices such as deep breathing, meditation, and mindfulness can help manage the physical and emotional symptoms of anxiety.

- Seeking Support: Sometimes, it may be beneficial to seek support from teachers, counselors, or mental health professionals, especially if test anxiety is severe.

Strategies to Overcome Anxiety

Anxiety, especially in the context of taking important tests like the HSPT, can significantly impact performance. It's crucial to develop strategies to manage and overcome this anxiety. Here's a deeper look into effective strategies:

Thorough Preparation:

- Foundation: Anxiety often stems from a fear of the unknown or feeling unprepared. Building a solid foundation through thorough study and understanding of the material is key.

- Regular Practice: Regular practice, including taking practice tests under timed conditions, can familiarize you with the test format and types of questions, reducing the fear of encountering surprises on the actual test day.

Relaxation Techniques:

- Deep Breathing: Simple yet effective, deep breathing can help calm the nervous system. Techniques like the 4-7-8 breathing method (inhale for 4 seconds, hold for 7 seconds, exhale for 8 seconds) are useful.

- Mindfulness and Meditation: Regular practice of mindfulness and meditation can help center your thoughts, reducing anxiety and improving concentration.

- Progressive Muscle Relaxation: This involves tensing and then relaxing different muscle groups in your body, which can reduce physical symptoms of stress and anxiety.

Positive Visualization:

- Mental Rehearsal: Imagine going through the motions of taking the test successfully. Visualization can help create a sense of familiarity and confidence.

- Success Imagery: Visualize not just the process, but also the successful outcome – completing the test confidently.

Self-Affirmation:

- Positive Self-Talk: Replace negative thoughts with positive affirmations. Remind yourself of your preparation and past successes.

- Building Confidence: Affirmations can help shift your mindset from doubt to confidence.

Setting Realistic Goals:

- Manageable Objectives: Set specific, achievable goals for both your preparation and performance on the test.

- Feedback-Based Adjustments: Regularly assess your progress and adjust your goals as necessary.

Embracing Mistakes as Learning Opportunities:

- Growth Mindset: Adopt the perspective that mistakes are an opportunity for learning, not a reflection of failure.
- Analyzing Errors: Understand why mistakes were made and how to avoid them in the future, which can reduce anxiety about repeating them.

Lifestyle Factors:

- Physical Exercise: Regular physical activity can reduce stress and anxiety levels.
- Adequate Sleep: Ensure you get enough rest. Sleep plays a crucial role in cognitive functions and emotional regulation.
- Balanced Nutrition: A healthy diet can impact your overall well-being, including stress levels.

Seeking Support:

- Discussion and Sharing: Sometimes, talking about your anxiety with someone you trust can provide relief and perspective.
- Professional Help: If anxiety becomes overwhelming, seeking help from a counselor or therapist can be beneficial.

Maintaining a Positive Mindset

Maintaining a positive mindset, especially in the context of preparing for and taking a challenging test like the HSPT, is crucial for optimal performance. A positive mindset can influence not only how you approach studying but also how you handle the pressure of the actual exam day. Here's a detailed exploration of how to maintain this mindset:

1. Understanding the Impact of Attitude:

- Mindset and Performance: Your mental attitude has a direct impact on your performance. A positive mindset can lead to better focus, greater motivation, and resilience in the face of challenges.
- Stress and Cognition: Negative stress or a pessimistic outlook can cloud judgment and impair cognitive functions like memory and concentration. Recognizing this can help you prioritize maintaining positivity.

2. Cultivating Positivity:

- Positive Self-Talk: Regularly engage in positive self-talk. Remind yourself of your strengths and past successes. Replace negative thoughts like "I can't do this" with affirmations like "I am prepared and capable."

- Focus on Progress, Not Perfection: Concentrate on the progress you are making rather than fixating on perfection. Celebrate small victories and improvements as they come.

3. Setting Realistic Expectations:

- Achievable Goals: Set realistic and achievable goals for both your preparation and the test itself. This helps create a sense of accomplishment and avoids feelings of inadequacy or failure.

- Preparation Confidence: Understand that thorough preparation will naturally lead to confidence. Trust in the work and effort you have put into studying.

4. Building Resilience:

- Embracing Challenges: View challenging topics or practice tests as opportunities to grow and learn, rather than as threats. This mindset shift can reduce anxiety and increase your ability to tackle difficult questions.

- Learning from Mistakes: Treat mistakes as learning opportunities. Analyzing why a mistake was made is often more educational than getting an answer correct.

5. Supportive Environment:

- Seek Support: Surround yourself with supportive people – friends, family, teachers – who encourage and believe in your abilities.

- Positive Affiliations: Engage in study groups or forums where you can share experiences and strategies with others preparing for the HSPT.

6. Visualization and Reflection:

- Positive Visualization: Regularly visualize a positive outcome, such as successfully completing the test. Visualization can condition your mind for success.

- Reflective Practice: Reflect on your study sessions and identify what went well. This reinforces a positive attitude towards your abilities and preparation.

7. Healthy Lifestyle:

- Physical Health: Regular exercise, a healthy diet, and adequate sleep significantly contribute to a positive mindset. Physical well-being is closely linked to mental well-being.

- Mindfulness and Relaxation: Practices such as meditation, yoga, or even simple breathing exercises can help maintain a calm and positive mindset.

Staying Calm and Focused During Preparation

Maintaining calmness and focus during the preparation phase for a significant test like the HSPT is essential. This state of mind not only enhances your ability to absorb and retain information but also sets the stage for how you handle the pressure during the actual exam. Let's delve into strategies to stay calm and focused during your preparation:

Develop a Structured Study Plan:

- Consistency Over Intensity: Instead of prolonged, intense study sessions, opt for a consistent, manageable schedule. Break down your study material into smaller, achievable tasks and set regular study times.

- Realistic Goals: Set realistic, clear goals for each study session. Achieving these smaller goals can boost your confidence and provide a sense of accomplishment.

Creating an Optimal Study Environment:

- Distraction-Free Zone: Choose a study area free from distractions. This might mean finding a quiet room, turning off unnecessary electronic devices, or informing others of your study schedule.

- Organized Space: Keep your study space organized. A clutter-free environment can help in reducing stress and keeping you focused.

Incorporating Breaks and Relaxation Techniques:

- Regular Breaks: Schedule short breaks during your study sessions. Use this time to stretch, take a walk, or engage in a relaxing activity. This helps in preventing burnout and keeps your mind fresh.

- Mindfulness and Meditation: Practice mindfulness or meditation techniques. Even a few minutes of deep breathing or guided relaxation can significantly reduce stress levels.

Maintaining Physical Health:

- Balanced Diet: Eating a balanced diet is crucial. Nutritious food provides the energy and concentration needed for effective studying.
- Regular Exercise: Incorporate regular physical activity into your routine. Exercise is a great stress reliever and improves mental clarity.
- Adequate Sleep: Ensure you get enough sleep. A well-rested mind is more efficient in learning and memory retention.

Positive Mindset:

- Self-Encouragement: Engage in positive self-talk. Remind yourself of your capabilities and past successes.
- Visualize Success: Spend time visualizing a successful outcome. This can be a powerful motivator and stress reliever.

Avoiding Cramming:

- Steady Review: Instead of cramming, focus on a steady review of material. This approach is more effective for long-term retention and understanding.
- Focus on Weak Areas: Use your study time to focus on areas where you feel less confident. Strengthening these areas can reduce anxiety.

Seek Support When Needed:

- Study Groups: Joining a study group can provide moral support and help clarify difficult concepts.
- Guidance from Teachers or Tutors: Don't hesitate to seek help from teachers or tutors if you're struggling with certain topics.

On the Exam Day

Exam day can be a critical moment for students, and how you approach this day can significantly impact your performance. Here's an expanded look at strategies and best practices for the day of the HSPT, focusing on mental preparation, practical steps, and maintaining focus and calmness during the exam.

1. Preparing the Night Before:

- Restful Sleep: Ensure a good night's sleep. This means avoiding last-minute cramming and instead opting for a relaxing evening. Adequate sleep is crucial for cognitive function and concentration.
- Gathering Necessary Materials: Prepare all the items you'll need for the exam (e.g., pens, pencils, erasers, ID, admission ticket) the night before to avoid morning rush and potential stress.

2. Morning of the Exam:

- Healthy Breakfast: Eat a nutritious breakfast. Foods that are high in protein and low in sugar are ideal as they provide sustained energy without the crash of high-sugar foods.
- Arriving Early: Plan to arrive at the exam center early to avoid the stress of being late. This extra time can help you to settle and adapt to the exam environment.

3. Establishing a Pre-Exam Routine:

- Relaxation Techniques: Engage in a short relaxation routine, whether it's deep breathing, mindfulness meditation, or gentle stretching. This can help in reducing anxiety and improving focus.
- Mental Preparation: Spend a few minutes mentally preparing yourself. This might involve going over your test-taking strategy or engaging in positive self-talk to boost your confidence.

4. During the Exam:

- Careful Reading of Instructions and Questions: Take the time to carefully read all instructions and questions to ensure you understand what is being asked.
- Time Management: Keep an eye on the clock, but don't let it pressure you. Plan your time wisely, allocating more time to questions that are worth more points or that you find more challenging.
- Staying Hydrated: If allowed, have water at your desk. Staying hydrated can help maintain concentration levels.
- Dealing with Anxiety: If you start to feel anxious during the exam, pause for a moment. Close your eyes, take a few deep breaths, and then refocus on the task at hand.

- Navigating Difficult Questions: If you encounter difficult questions, don't dwell on them for too long. Mark them and move on; you can always return to them later if time permits.

5. Post-Exam Protocol:

- Avoiding Post-Exam Discussions: Right after the exam, it's often best to avoid detailed discussions about the questions with peers, as this can sometimes lead to unnecessary stress or second-guessing.

- Reflection and Relaxation: Reflect on your performance in a constructive way, noting areas for future improvement. Then, allow yourself some time to relax and unwind.

PRACTICE TEST 1

1. Verbal Skills

Analogies

1. Hand is to Glove as Foot is to:
   A) Sock B) Shoe C) Sandal D) Toe

2. Whisper is to Shout as Murmur is to: A) Talk B) Yell C) Hum D) Mumble

3. Writer is to Pen as Painter is to: A) Brush B) Canvas C) Easel D) Art

4. Water is to Ice as Steam is to: A) Heat B) Condensation C) Vapor D) Boiling

5. Quiet is to Silent as Dim is to: A) Dark B) Light C) Shadow D) Twilight

6. Seed is to Plant as Egg is to: A) Chicken B) Nest C) Birth D) Hatch

7. Chef is to Kitchen as Pilot is to: A) Airport B) Airplane C) Flight D) Control Tower

8. Actor is to Script as Musician is to: A) Instrument B) Concert C) Song D) Score

9. Cup is to Coffee as Bowl is to: A) Dish B) Soup C) Spoon D) Table

10. Library is to Books as Orchard is to: A) Trees B) Fruits C) Leaves D) Branches

11. Day is to Night as Dawn is to: A) Evening B) Dusk C) Noon D) Sunrise

12. Shield is to Protection as Medicine is to: A) Health B) Doctor C) Cure D) Illness

Synonyms

1. Choose the word that is most similar in meaning to: **Obstinate** A) Flexible B) Stubborn C) Yielding D) Willing

2. Choose the word that is most similar in meaning to: **Benevolent** A) Malevolent B) Kind C) Indifferent D) Cruel

3. Choose the word that is most similar in meaning to: **Capricious** A) Predictable B) Unchanging C) Whimsical D) Steady

4. Choose the word that is most similar in meaning to: **Desolate** A) Populated B) Barren C) Crowded D) Fertile

5. Choose the word that is most similar in meaning to: **Vivacious** A) Lively B) Dull C) Morose D) Depressed

6. Choose the word that is most similar in meaning to: **Melancholy** A) Joyful B) Elated C) Somber D) Excited

7. Choose the word that is most similar in meaning to: **Opulent** A) Poor B) Lavish C) Sparse D) Economical

8. Choose the word that is most similar in meaning to: **Perilous** A) Safe B) Dangerous C) Protected D) Secure

9. Choose the word that is most similar in meaning to: **Covert** A) Open B) Secretive C) Visible D) Obvious

10. Choose the word that is most similar in meaning to: **Ardent** A) Apathetic B) Passionate C) Indifferent D) Dispassionate

11. Choose the word that is most similar in meaning to: **Candid** A) Deceptive B) Forthright C) Secretive D) Dishonest

12. Choose the word that is most similar in meaning to: **Quaint** A) Modern B) Charming C) Usual D) Standard

Antonyms

1. Choose the word that is most opposite in meaning to: **Abundant** A) Scarce B) Ample C) Plentiful D) Sufficient

2. Choose the word that is most opposite in meaning to: **Elevate** A) Ascend B) Rise C) Lower D) Soar

3. Choose the word that is most opposite in meaning to: **Compliment** A) Flatter B) Praise C) Criticize D) Approve

4. Choose the word that is most opposite in meaning to: **Harmony** A) Peace B) Discord C) Agreement D) Accord

5. Choose the word that is most opposite in meaning to: **Optimistic** A) Hopeful B) Confident C) Pessimistic D) Positive

6. Choose the word that is most opposite in meaning to: **Conceal** A) Hide B) Veil C) Reveal D) Cover

7. Choose the word that is most opposite in meaning to: **Expand** A) Enlarge B) Extend C) Contract D) Inflate

8. Choose the word that is most opposite in meaning to: **Ancient** A) Old B) Modern C) Archaic D) Antiquated

9. Choose the word that is most opposite in meaning to: **Rigid** A) Stiff B) Flexible C) Hard D) Inflexible

10. Choose the word that is most opposite in meaning to: **Thrifty** A) Economical B) Frugal C) Wasteful D) Careful

11. Choose the word that is most opposite in meaning to: **Transparent** A) Clear B) Opaque C) Visible D) Lucid

12. Choose the word that is most opposite in meaning to: **Mend** A) Repair B) Break C) Fix D) Heal

Logic

1. If all A are B, and all B are C, which must be true? A) All C are A B) Some A are C C) No A are C D) All A are C

2. If no M are N, and all N are O, which is true? A) Some O are not M B) All M are O C) No M are O D) All O are M

3. If some X are Y, and no Y are Z, which is possible? A) All X are Z B) Some X are not Z C) No X are Z D) All of the above

4. Only students who study well will pass the HSPT. Maria did not pass the HSPT. Therefore: A) Maria is not a student. B) Maria studied well. C) Maria did not study well. D) Maria will study well in the future.

5. Every time it rains, the ground gets wet. The ground is not wet. Therefore: A) It did not rain. B) It might rain. C) It rained. D) The ground absorbs water quickly.

6. All good athletes are disciplined. Some disciplined people are not athletes. Therefore: A) Some athletes are not disciplined. B) All disciplined people are good athletes. C) Some good athletes are not disciplined. D) Discipline is not required to be a good athlete.

7. Either the book is on the shelf, or it is on the table. The book is not on the shelf. Therefore: A) The book is on the table. B) The book is lost. C) The book cannot be on the table. D) The book might be on the shelf.

8. No birds are dogs, and all dogs are mammals. Therefore: A) Some mammals are not birds. B) All birds are mammals. C) No birds are mammals. D) Some birds are not mammals.

9. If it is summer, then the days are long. It is not summer. Therefore: A) The days are short. B) The days might be long. C) It can never be summer. D) The days are not long.

10. All squares are rectangles, but not all rectangles are squares. You see a rectangle. Therefore: A) It must be a square. B) It might be a square. C) It cannot be a square. D) It is not a rectangle.

11. If a plant is a rose, it has thorns. This plant does not have thorns. Therefore: A) It is not a rose. B) It might be a rose. C) It is a rose. D) Roses do not have thorns.

12. Every cat has a tail. This animal does not have a tail. Therefore: A) This animal is a cat. B) This animal is not a cat. C) All animals have tails. D) Some cats do not have tails.

Verbal Classifications

For each question, choose the word that does not belong with the others.

1. A) Sparrow B) Eagle C) Robin D) Frog
2. A) Basketball B) Baseball C) Soccer D) Chess
3. A) Rose B) Tulip C) Daffodil D) Cactus
4. A) Hammer B) Nail C) Screwdriver D) Wrench
5. A) Monday B) Thursday C) Sunday D) Weekday
6. A) Guitar B) Violin C) Flute D) Piano
7. A) Red B) Blue C) Green D) Color
8. A) Copper B) Iron C) Steel D) Silver
9. A) River B) Lake C) Ocean D) Pool
10. A) Novel B) Poem C) Biography D) Fiction
11. A) Carrot B) Potato C) Tomato D) Broccoli
12. A) Circle B) Triangle C) Square D) Line

2.Quantitative Skills

Number Series

For each number series, identify the next number in the sequence.

1. 2, 4, 6, 8, ?
2. 1, 4, 9, 16, ?
3. 5, 10, 20, 40, ?
4. 1, 1, 2, 3, 5, ?
5. 10, 8, 6, 4, ?
6. 2, 6, 18, 54, ?
7. 100, 90, 80, 70, ?
8. 3, 9, 27, 81, ?
9. 1, 2, 4, 8, 16, ?
10. 21, 18, 15, 12, ?
11. 1, 3, 6, 10, 15, ?
12. 14, 28, 56, 112, ?
13. 2, 3, 5, 9, 17, ?

Geometric Comparisons

1. Two triangles are similar. The first triangle has a side length of 5 cm. If the corresponding side length of the second triangle is 10 cm, what is the ratio of their areas?
2. A square and a rectangle have the same perimeter. If the square has a side length of 6 cm, and the rectangle has a length of 10 cm, what is the width of the rectangle?
3. A circle and a square have the same area. What is the ratio of the side length of the square to the diameter of the circle?
4. Two cylinders have the same height. If the radius of the first cylinder is half the radius of the second cylinder, how do their volumes compare?
5. If two cubes have volumes in the ratio 1:8, how do the lengths of their edges compare?

6. Two rectangles have the same area of 36 cm². If one has a length that is twice its width and the other has a length that is thrice its width, what are the dimensions of each rectangle?

7. A right triangle has legs of 3 cm and 4 cm. A second triangle has sides of the same length as the hypotenuse of the first. Which triangle has a larger area?

8. A circle has a circumference that is twice the length of the side of a square. Which has a greater area, the circle or the square?

9. Two trapezoids have the same height. The first trapezoid has bases of 4 cm and 6 cm, and the second has bases of 5 cm and 7 cm. Which trapezoid has a larger area?

10. A regular hexagon and an equilateral triangle have the same perimeter. Which shape has a larger area?

11. Two cones have the same volume. If the radius of the first cone is twice that of the second cone, what is the relationship between their heights?

12. A rectangular prism has a length of 8 cm, a width of 3 cm, and a height of 2 cm. A cylinder has a diameter of 6 cm and the same height as the prism. Which has a larger volume?

13. An equilateral triangle and a square are inscribed in the same circle. Which shape has a larger perimeter?

Non-Geometric Comparisons

For each question, determine if Quantity A is greater than, less than, or equal to Quantity B.

1. Quantity A: The number of minutes in 2 hours Quantity B: The number of minutes in 120 minutes

2. Quantity A: Half of 150 Quantity B: One third of 225

3. Quantity A: The result of multiplying 0.25 by 100 Quantity B: The result of dividing 25 by 1

4. Quantity A: The sum of the digits in the number 505 Quantity B: The sum of the digits in the number 550

5. Quantity A: The number of seconds in 10 minutes Quantity B: The number of seconds in 600 seconds

6. Quantity A: The square of 12 Quantity B: The square root of 144

7. Quantity A: The product of 7 and 8 Quantity B: The product of 14 and 4

8. Quantity A: 1/2 of 100 Quantity B: 1/4 of 400

9. Quantity A: 20% of 50 Quantity B: 25% of 40

10. Quantity A: The remainder when 50 is divided by 6 Quantity B: The remainder when 81 is divided by 8

11. Quantity A: The number of edges on a cube Quantity B: The number of corners on a cube

12. Quantity A: The number of days in three weeks Quantity B: The number of days in 21 days

13. Quantity A: The sum of all even numbers between 1 and 10 (inclusive) Quantity B: The sum of all odd numbers between 1 and 10 (inclusive)

Number Manipulations

1. If you add 6 to a number and then double the result, you get 20. What is the original number?

2. Subtract 3 from a number, then multiply the result by 5, and you get 35. What is the number?

3. Divide a number by 4 and then add 12 to get a result of 20. What is the original number?

4. Multiply a number by 3 and then subtract 5 to get 28. What is the number?

5. The product of a number and 7 is 84. What is the number?

6. If you square a number and then subtract 9, the result is 16. What is the original number?

7. When a number is increased by 15%, the result is 115. What is the original number?

8. If you divide a number by half and then add 10, you get 30. What is the original number?

9. A number decreased by 20% is 80. What is the original number?

10. The sum of a number and its reciprocal is 13/6. What is the number?

11. If you subtract a number from its square, the result is 30. What is the number?

12. A number is divided into two parts in a ratio of 3:2. If the larger part is 18, what is the smaller part?

13. When 44 is added to a number, the result is the same as squaring the number. What is the number?

3.Reading Comprehension

Main Idea

Passage:

Jupiter's moon Io is the most volcanically active body in the solar system. With over 400 active volcanoes covering its relatively small surface area, Io boasts more volcanic activity than even Earth. This extreme volcanism is the result of gravitational forces from Jupiter and other neighboring moons, which stretch and flex Io's interior, generating tremendous internal heat.

The predominant type of volcanism on Io consists of continually erupting lava fountains, lakes, and flows. Unlike terrestrial volcanoes which may erupt sporadically and then remain dormant for a long time, Ionian volcanic plumes are essentially always active once they form. This creates sprawling lava flows and lakes as fluid rock constantly pours from volcanic vents. The largest of these fiery lakes, Loki Patera, is around 154 miles in diameter, making it bigger than Lake Michigan.

Io's violent volcanism leads to a constantly renewing surface as new volcanic deposits resurface large portions of the moon. Within a timeframe of about a million years, which is short on a geological scale, the surface can be completely resurfaced in places. The consequences are a lack of older surface features and extremely dynamic landforms as lava flows reshape the landscape. Some mountains on Io are isolated crystal towers rising like exotic islands in oceans of newly hardened lava. Exploring Io's volatile surface someday promises to reveal remarkable sights.

Questions:

1. What is the main idea of the first paragraph?
2. What is the main point being made in the second paragraph?
3. What is the passage's main idea about Io's volcanoes?
4. What main observation does the passage make by comparing Io to Earth?
5. What does the passage mainly suggest about Loki Patera?
6. What main reason does the passage give for Io's lack of older surface features?

7. The third paragraph mainly discusses what about Io's landscape?

8. What main comparison does the passage make with Lake Michigan? Why?

9. The crystal tower mountains are mainly mentioned to?

10. What main activity makes Io unique in the passage?

11. What evidence mainly supports Io being volcanically active?

12. What can readers mainly conclude is the source of Io's internal heat?

13. What does the passage mainly suggest exploring Io's surface would reveal?

Details

Passage:

The peregrine falcon is renowned for its speed and aerial acrobatics. As birds of prey go, few can match its hunting prowess. Reaching speeds of nearly 200 miles per hour when diving for prey, peregrines may be the fastest birds on Earth. With pointed wings and a streamlined body shape, they seem designed for their role as skilled hunters.

Peregrines hunt other birds in flight, using their incredible speed to overtake their prey. Before beginning a stoop, or dive, peregrines will climb high into the air, sometimes thousands of feet above the ground. From this vantage point, they scan below for potential prey, which includes smaller birds like pigeons, starlings, jays, and even ducks. Once spotted, the peregrines fold their wings and enter a steep dive towards their target. They strike their prey in mid-air with tremendous force, instantly killing or disabling it. The lifeless or stunned prey is then retrieved in flight and carried back to a nest or perch to be eaten. Even when not hunting, peregrines spend much of their time soaring to great heights and making aerial acrobatic moves at high speeds, seemingly just for enjoyment.

With wingspans typically around 3 to 4 feet across, peregrine falcons are formidable predators. Today, following near extinction in the mid-20th century and extensive conservation efforts, healthy populations of peregrines have rebounded in many regions. Seeing one perform its aerial feats remains an exciting experience for any birder.

Questions:

1. What speed can peregrine falcons reach when diving for prey?
2. What feature of the peregrine's body shape makes it well-suited for hunting?
3. What types of other birds do peregrines hunt?
4. About how high might peregrines climb when starting a hunting dive?
5. What hunting maneuver do peregrines use when diving for prey?
6. How do peregrines kill or stun their prey after striking it?
7. What do peregrines do with prey once it has been disabled or killed?
8. When might peregrines perform aerial acrobatics, according to the passage?
9. About how wide is an average peregrine falcon's wingspan?
10. What conservation efforts helped restore peregrine populations in recent decades?
11. What happened to peregrine populations in the mid-1900s, according to the passage?
12. Why might seeing a peregrine falcon hunt be exciting for a birder?
13. Which word means the opposite of 'lifeless'?

For each question, students would need to read the provided passage carefully to locate and understand specific facts or pieces of evidence presented by the author. This practice helps in honing the ability to focus on details, which is a crucial aspect of reading comprehension. It's important to note that while some details will be explicitly stated, others may require the reader to make inferences based on the given information. Students should practice skimming for keywords related to the questions and scanning for direct information to efficiently find details within the passage.

Inference

Passage:

Large and famously gregarious, humpback whales migrate longer distances than any other marine mammal, demonstrating a stunning feat of endurance and navigation. These 40- to 50-ton whales make epic round-trip voyages each year between their warm-water breeding grounds and colder, more productive feeding areas. Routes span thousands of miles across entire oceans.

Though humpbacks may travel in loose groups, they do not maintain prolonged social bonds as some whales do. Leading predominantly solitary lives, their chief interactions involve courting, calving, and competitive groups orchestrating complex songs needed to mate. Male humpbacks also duke it out among themselves once every other decade for an esteemed central position within a competitive group. Beyond these periodic interactions, solitary travel and hunting prevail.

Hunting strategies vary greatly between regions and focus on areas with dense prey concentrations. A common hunting style is bubble netting, where a blowhole exhalation traps fish inside rising bubbles. The trapping manuever requires no cooperation, reflecting the species' general lack thereof, but is more successful with greater individual experience and skill.

Humpbacks emit a diverse array of feeding calls that allow eavesdropping whales to locate promising areas from miles away. Their haunting song evolves gradually with exchanges between competitive groups each season. Humans have decoded some feeding calls but the song's intricate composition still perplexes scientists 50 years later. If nothing else, the song serves as a testament to the rich culture of this largely nomadic, independent species.

Questions:

1. Which aspect of humpback behavior suggests advanced intelligence?
2. What clue suggests the passage spans the months of least humpback food availability?
3. In what sense do humpbacks lead predominantly solitary lives?
4. About how heavy is a mature humpback whale?
5. How might a younger humpback benefit from the hunting skills of experienced adults?
6. How do humpbacks alert others to prime hunting areas from afar?
7. What role does competition play in a humpback whale's life?
8. How might the humpback's haunting song prove beneficial?

9. Why might humpbacks have less need of group cooperation than some marine mammals?

10. What do the complex song and strategic hunting abilities suggest about humpbacks?

11. What protective purpose might periodic aggressive displays between males have?

12. How have scientists failed to fully understand humpback whale songs?

13. Which word suggests transitional lifestyle changes across generations?

For inference questions, students must read between the lines, using clues and evidence from the text to draw conclusions about things not directly stated. This involves understanding subtleties, recognizing tone, and interpreting the broader context provided by the author. It is important for students to combine their own knowledge and reasoning with the information provided to answer these types of questions.

Vocabulary

Passage:

The onset of the Little Ice Age profoundly impacted human civilization from the 14th to 19th centuries with severe cooling leading to chaotic climate disruptions. While several factors probably contributed, reduced solar activity during this 500-year period dealt the sharpest blow in throttling global warmth. Interacting ocean and atmospheric changes amplified solar influences to spur a temperature rollercoaster marked by extreme weather and environmental anomalies on a seesawing timescale.

The Northern Hemisphere bore the brunt as growing seasons shrank drastically, ushering waves of food shortages, famines, and disease. Iceland's Vatnajökull glacier surged as pack ice choked coastal waters, decimating fishing industries. Alpine glaciers claimed farms and villages. Years with incessant rains rendered soils sodden and unsuitable for crops, while droughts alternated unpredictably.

River turbulence surged. The Little Ice Age's autumn severity delayed freeze-up while spring melts accelerated, boosting river flows across seasons. Peak flood stages grew increasingly volatile, engulfing drainage infrastructure. Combined with violent oceanic storms riding North Atlantic currents, raging rivers reshaped human settlement patterns across Europe.

The Little Ice Age delivers lasting lessons on societal fragility in the face of climate upheaval. While gradual warming thereafter stimulated positive change, the period's tumults dealt sharp blows to developing nations. It embodies ongoing challenges communities worldwide face amid shifting weather extremes wrought by modern climate change. Its study remains profoundly instructive.

Questions:

1. Which word means a waterway?
2. What does onset mean?
3. Which phrase means very cold?
4. What does the word ample mean? Find a synonym.
5. What does the passage mean by a "temperature rollercoaster"?
6. Which word phrase means fitting together tightly?
7. What does the word sodden mean?
8. What does turbulence refer to?
9. What does the word volatile mean?
10. What does the phrase "riding oceanic currents" convey about storms?
11. What does the word embodies mean?
12. What does the word thereafter mean?
13. Which phrase means instructive or educational?

Conclusion

Passage:

Many designs claiming to be solar powered watches do not actually use sunlight as their primary power source. Rather, they require routine battery changes to recharge small photovoltaic cells that in reality contribute marginal supplemental energy. By contrast, a true solar watch relies predominantly on converted sunlight for all of its operations.

A solar watch utilizes photovoltaic panels on its dial to capture light and generate electrical currents. This electricity is stored within an integrated rechargeable battery, which powers the watch. Efficiency levels vary, but a quality solar timepiece needs occasional light exposure rather than battery replacements to continually recharge its vital operations.

Crystal, dial, and movement designs merit equal consideration as efficiency factors when evaluating solar watches. Clear crystals above clean watch dials optimize light capture. Efficient movements also conserve energy consumption between charging periods. These elements distinguish a genuine solar watch engineered to extract a self-sustaining energy cycle during everyday use conditions.

In summary, while all watches labeled solar contain photovoltaic cells, only a select tier operates predominantly on solar energy. Carefully inspect labeled watches when sources claim true solar-powered functionality. Seek displays verifying regular use absent battery changes, backed by optimized solar harvesting visible across key components. If doubts persist, contact manufacturers directly for solar operational metrics. Thereby determine which timepieces actually thrive on rays from the sky rather than those perpetually hungry for more.

Questions:

1. The author's view is that most watches claiming solar capabilities are what?
2. What does the passage suggest about the role batteries play in typical solar watches?
3. Based on the passage, why might occasional sun exposure be preferable to battery changes?

4. The passage suggests clear crystals and dials contribute to what?

5. Efficient movements likely help in what specific way?

6. What distinguishes a fully solar powered watch, according to the author?

7. What does the author suggest seeking out and inspecting carefully regarding solar watches?

8. What might directly contacting manufacturers reveal about their watches?

9. What does the passage conclude about true solar watches?

10. What judgment does the author convey about most so-called solar watches?

11. What tone does the author take regarding solar watch claims?

12. What advice does the author clearly favor over passive acceptance of solar claims?

13. Which choice best summarizes the passage's conclusion about solar watches?

4.Mathematics

Concepts

1. **Algebraic Concepts**:
   - Simplify the expression: $2(3x + 4) - 5x$.

2. **Geometric Concepts**:
   - If the angles of a triangle are in the ratio 2:3:4, what is the measure of the largest angle?

3. **Number Theory**:
   - What is the greatest common divisor (GCD) of 36 and 48?

4. **Probability**:
   - A bag contains 3 red, 2 blue, and 5 green marbles. What is the probability of randomly picking a green marble?

5. **Statistics**:
   - The mean of five numbers is 10. If four of the numbers are 8, 11, 9, and 12, what is the fifth number?

6. **Ratios and Proportions**:
   - If the ratio of boys to girls in a class is 3:4 and there are 12 boys, how many girls are there?

7. **Linear Equations**:
   - Solve for y in the equation: $2y - 4 = 10$.

8. **Quadratic Equations**:
   - What are the solutions to the equation $x^2 - 5x + 6 = 0$?

9. **Functions**:
   - If $f(x) = 3x + 2$, find $f(5)$.

10. **Geometry – Circles**:
    - Find the circumference of a circle with a radius of 7 cm (use $\pi = 3.14$).

11. **Trigonometry**:
    - What is the sine of 30 degrees?

12. **Systems of Equations**:
    - Solve the system of equations: $y = 2x + 3$ and $y = -x + 7$.

13. **Percentage**:

- What is 20% of 150?

Problem-Solving

1. A train travels 180 miles in 3 hours. At the same speed, how far will it travel in 5 hours?
2. If 5 pencils cost $1.25, how much do 12 pencils cost?
3. A rectangle has a length of 15 cm and a width that is 3 cm less. What is the area of the rectangle?
4. A car's gas tank holds 20 gallons. If the car gets 30 miles per gallon, how far can it travel on a full tank?
5. If 3 apples and 4 oranges cost $2, and 4 apples and 3 oranges cost $1.75, how much does one apple cost?
6. A rectangular garden measures 20 feet by 30 feet. If a fence is built around the perimeter, how many feet of fencing is needed?
7. An object is thrown upward with an initial velocity of 40 meters per second. How long will it take to hit the ground? (Ignore air resistance and use g = 10 m/s² for gravity.)
8. If the sum of three consecutive even numbers is 54, what is the smallest of these numbers?
9. A store offers a 15% discount on an item priced at $200. What is the sale price after the discount?
10. A baker uses 2 cups of flour for every 1 cup of sugar. If the baker has 10 cups of flour, how many cups of sugar are needed?
11. A clock shows 3:15. What is the angle between the hour and minute hands?
12. A school buys tablets at $250 each and sells them at a 20% profit. What is the selling price per tablet?
13. If water is dripping from a tap at a rate of 6 drops per minute, how many drops will have dripped in 3 hours?

Arithmetic

1. **Addition**: What is the sum of 123 and 456?
2. **Subtraction**: Subtract 321 from 789.
3. **Multiplication**: Multiply 24 by 15.
4. **Division**: Divide 144 by 12.
5. **Fractions**: What is 1/2 of 3/4?
6. **Decimals**: Add 2.5 and 3.75.
7. **Percentage**: What is 25% of 200?
8. **Mixed Operations**: Evaluate 3(5 + 2) - 4.
9. **Long Division**: Divide 12345 by 123.
10. **Fraction to Decimal**: Convert 3/8 to a decimal.
11. **Decimal to Percentage**: Convert 0.75 to a percentage.
12. **Comparing Fractions**: Which is greater, 1/2 or 2/3?
13. **Rounding Numbers**: Round 5.786 to the nearest tenth.

Algebra

1. Solve for x: x + 5 = 12
2. Simplify the expression: 2x - 3x + 4
3. Solve for y: 3y - 5 = 10
4. Factorize the expression: x^2 - 9
5. Solve the quadratic equation: x^2 - 5x + 6 = 0
6. Simplify: (2x + 3)(x - 4)
7. Solve for z: 2z/3 = 8
8. Expand and simplify: (x + 3)(x - 2)
9. Solve for w: w/5 + 6 = 9
10. Factorize completely: $6x^2$ - 12x
11. Solve for t: 4t + 5 = 3t + 10
12. Solve the system of equations: y = 2x + 3 and y = x + 5
13. Solve for a: 5(a - 2) = 2a + 6

Geometry

1. Calculate the area of a rectangle with a length of 8 cm and a width of 3 cm.

2. What is the perimeter of a square with a side length of 5 meters?

3. Find the volume of a cube with edge length 4 inches.

4. What is the measure of each angle in an equilateral triangle?

5. Calculate the area of a circle with a radius of 7 cm (use $\pi = 3.14$).

6. A right triangle has one leg that measures 6 cm and a hypotenuse of 10 cm. Find the length of the other leg.

7. What is the total surface area of a cylinder with a radius of 3 cm and a height of 5 cm (use $\pi = 3.14$)?

8. Find the measure of the missing angle in a triangle with angles of 35 degrees and 85 degrees.

9. Calculate the circumference of a circle with a diameter of 8 inches (use $\pi = 3.14$).

10. A parallelogram has base lengths of 10 cm and height 7 cm. What is its area?

11. How many diagonals does a regular hexagon have?

12. What is the volume of a rectangular prism with dimensions 8 cm, 5 cm, and 2 cm?

13. Find the length of the arc of a circle with a radius of 10 cm subtended by a central angle of 30 degrees (use $\pi = 3.14$).

5. Language Skills –

Punctuation

1. **Choose the sentence with the correct use of commas**:
   - A) After dinner, I'll go jogging.
   - B) After dinner I'll go, jogging.

2. **Identify the sentence with the correct placement of the apostrophe**:
   - A) The childrens' toys were scattered everywhere.
   - B) The children's toys were scattered everywhere.

3. **Choose the sentence that correctly uses a semicolon**:
   - A) She loves reading; she reads every day.
   - B) She loves reading; and she reads every day.

4. **Select the sentence with the correct use of colons**:
   - A) She brought all she needed: a flashlight, a tent, and a sleeping bag.
   - B) She brought: a flashlight, a tent, and a sleeping bag.

5. **Identify the sentence with correct hyphenation**:
   - A) The well-known author was visiting our school.
   - B) The well known author was visiting our school.

6. **Choose the correct usage of quotation marks**:
   - A) "I can't wait for the weekend", she said.
   - B) "I can't wait for the weekend," she said.

7. **Identify the sentence with correct ellipsis usage**:
   - A) I don't know... maybe I'll go.
   - B) I don't know. Maybe... I'll go.

8. **Select the sentence with the correct use of parentheses**:
   - A) He finally answered (after taking five minutes to think) and said yes.
   - B) He finally answered (after taking five minutes to think and said yes).

9. **Choose the sentence with the correct use of exclamation marks**:
   - A) Wow! That was an amazing performance.
   - B) Wow! that was an amazing performance.

10. **Identify the sentence with the correct use of dashes**:

- A) My favorite activities - running, swimming, and biking - are all outdoors.
- B) My favorite activities - running, swimming and biking are all outdoors.

11. **Choose the correct usage of question marks**:
    - A) Will you come with me? She asked.
    - B) "Will you come with me?" she asked.

12. **Select the sentence with the correct use of brackets**:
    - A) He finally understood the concept [of quantum mechanics].
    - B) He finally understood [the concept of quantum mechanics].

Usage

1. **Choose the sentence with the correct verb tense**:
    - A) She writes a letter every day.
    - B) She write a letter every day.

2. **Identify the sentence with correct subject-verb agreement**:
    - A) The team is playing well.
    - B) The team are playing well.

3. **Choose the correct pronoun usage**:
    - A) Between you and I, this is a secret.
    - B) Between you and me, this is a secret.

4. **Select the sentence with the correct adjective usage**:
    - A) She felt badly about the mistake.
    - B) She felt bad about the mistake.

5. **Choose the sentence with the correct adverb placement**:
    - A) He runs quickly.
    - B) He quickly runs.

6. **Identify the sentence with correct preposition usage**:
    - A) He insisted on paying for the dinner.
    - B) He insisted in paying for the dinner.

7. **Choose the correct conjunction usage**:

- A) She wanted to go to the park, but it was raining.
- B) She wanted to go to the park, and it was raining.

8. **Select the sentence with correct word choice**:
   - A) The dessert was complemented with a sweet wine.
   - B) The dessert was complimented with a sweet wine.

9. **Identify the sentence with the correct article usage**:
   - A) An apple a day keeps the doctor away.
   - B) A apple a day keeps the doctor away.

10. **Choose the sentence with the correct use of modifiers**:
    - A) The dog chased the boy with a stick.
    - B) The dog with a stick chased the boy.

11. **Select the sentence with correct capitalization**:
    - A) I visited the Eiffel Tower in Paris.
    - B) I visited the eiffel tower in Paris.

12. **Choose the correct plural form**:
    - A) There are many cactuses in the desert.
    - B) There are many cacti in the desert.

13. **Identify the sentence with correct passive voice usage**:
    - A) The book was read by her in one day.
    - B) The book was read in one day by her.

Spelling

1. **Choose the correctly spelled word**:
   - A) Acommodate
   - B) Accommodate

2. **Identify the word with the correct spelling**:
   - A) Seperate
   - B) Separate

3. **Choose the correctly spelled word**:
   - A) Priviledge
   - B) Privilege

4. **Select the word with the correct spelling**:
   - A) Concensus
   - B) Consensus

5. **Choose the correctly spelled word**:
   - A) Existance
   - B) Existence

6. **Identify the word with the correct spelling**:
   - A) Millenium
   - B) Millennium

7. **Choose the correctly spelled word**:
   - A) Embarass
   - B) Embarrass

8. **Select the word with the correct spelling**:
   - A) Occurence
   - B) Occurrence

9. **Choose the correctly spelled word**:
   - A) Supersede
   - B) Supercede

10. **Identify the word with the correct spelling**:
    - A) Liaison
    - B) Liason

11. **Choose the correctly spelled word**:
    - A) Calendar
    - B) Calender

12. **Select the word with the correct spelling**:
    - A) Maintainance
    - B) Maintenance

13. **Choose the correctly spelled word**:
    - A) Definately
    - B) Definitely

Capitalization

Choose the sentence with correct capitalization:

A) I will visit the Grand Canyon in July.

B) I will visit the grand canyon in July.

Identify the correct capitalization:

A) The President will address the nation tonight.

B) The president will address the nation tonight.

Select the sentence with proper capitalization:

A) She studied biology and chemistry at the university.

B) She studied Biology and Chemistry at the University.

Choose the correctly capitalized sentence:

A) We watched the Sunrise from the east coast.

B) We watched the sunrise from the East Coast.

Identify the sentence with correct capitalization:

A) My Aunt and Uncle live in Texas.

B) My aunt and uncle live in Texas.

Select the sentence with proper capitalization:

A) The river Thames flows through London.

B) The River Thames flows through London.

Choose the correctly capitalized sentence:

A) Did you see the Full moon last night?

B) Did you see the full moon last night?

Identify the sentence with correct capitalization:

A) The Eiffel Tower is located in Paris, France.

B) The eiffel tower is located in Paris, France.

Select the sentence with proper capitalization:

A) The book was titled "Journey to the West."

B) The book was titled "Journey To The West."

Choose the correctly capitalized sentence:

A) The CEO of the company will speak at the event.

B) The Ceo of the company will speak at the event.

Identify the sentence with correct capitalization:

A) The Doctor will see you now.

B) The doctor will see you now.

Select the sentence with proper capitalization:

A) This winter, we will vacation in the Rocky Mountains.

B) This Winter, we will vacation in the rocky mountains.

Choose the correctly capitalized sentence:

A) The Statue of Liberty is an iconic landmark.

B) The statue of liberty is an iconic landmark.

Grammar

1. **Choose the sentence with correct subject-verb agreement**:
   - A) The committee meets regularly.
   - B) The committee meet regularly.
2. **Identify the sentence with the correct verb tense**:
   - A) We had dinner when he arrived.
   - B) We have had dinner when he arrived.
3. **Select the sentence with proper pronoun usage**:
   - A) Her and I went to the store.
   - B) She and I went to the store.

4. **Choose the sentence with correct preposition usage**:
   - A) She is interested on learning Spanish.
   - B) She is interested in learning Spanish.

5. **Identify the sentence with correct modifier placement**:
   - A) The girl almost cried watching the movie four times.
   - B) The girl watched the movie almost four times and cried.

6. **Select the sentence with proper conjunction usage**:
   - A) I will call you and I get home.
   - B) I will call you when I get home.

7. **Choose the sentence with correct article usage**:
   - A) An elephant and a mouse were friends.
   - B) An elephant and mouse were friends.

8. **Identify the sentence with correct adjective order**:
   - A) She wore a beautiful, long, red dress.
   - B) She wore a red, long, beautiful dress.

9. **Select the sentence with proper use of infinitives**:
   - A) To running is her favorite activity.
   - B) To run is her favorite activity.

10. **Choose the sentence with correct adverb usage**:
    - A) She sings beautifully.
    - B) She sings beautiful.

11. **Identify the sentence with correct passive voice usage**:
    - A) The cake was eaten by them.
    - B) The cake was eaten them.

12. **Select the sentence with proper use of gerunds**:
    - A) Swimming is my favorite sport.
    - B) To swim is my favorite sport.

13. **Choose the sentence with correct comparative and superlative usage**:
    - A) This is the more interesting book I've read.
    - B) This is the most interesting book I've read.

Answers and Explanations

VERBAL SKILLS

Analogies

1. **Question**: Hand is to Glove as Foot is to: **Answer**: B) Shoe **Explanation**: A glove is a piece of clothing that covers the hand, just as a shoe is a piece of clothing that covers the foot. Both are items of clothing designed specifically for the body part they cover.

2. **Question**: Whisper is to Shout as Murmur is to: **Answer**: B) Yell **Explanation**: Whispering and murmuring are both forms of speaking softly, whereas shouting and yelling are forms of speaking very loudly. The relationship here is the level of volume at which something is said.

3. **Question**: Writer is to Pen as Painter is to: **Answer**: A) Brush **Explanation**: A writer uses a pen as a primary tool for writing, and a painter uses a brush as a primary tool for painting. The relationship is that of a professional or craftsman to their tool of trade.

4. **Question**: Water is to Ice as Steam is to: **Answer**: C) Vapor **Explanation**: Water turns into ice when it freezes and into steam when it evaporates. Similarly, steam can refer to water vapor that is a gas form of water when it is heated.

5. **Question**: Quiet is to Silent as Dim is to: **Answer**: A) Dark **Explanation**: Quiet and dim both suggest a lesser degree of something (sound and light, respectively), whereas silent and dark suggest the absence or complete minimization of those same things.

6. **Question**: Seed is to Plant as Egg is to: **Answer**: A) Chicken **Explanation**: A seed is a small object that can grow into a plant, just as an egg is a small object that can develop into a chicken. The relationship is that of a beginning stage to its mature form.

7. **Question**: Chef is to Kitchen as Pilot is to: **Answer**: B) Airplane **Explanation**: A chef works in a kitchen, and a pilot works in an airplane. The relationship here is a professional to their place of work.

8. **Question**: Actor is to Script as Musician is to: **Answer**: D) Score **Explanation**: An actor uses a script to perform a role, just as a musician uses a score to perform music. The relationship is that of a performer to the material they use for their performance.

9. **Question**: Cup is to Coffee as Bowl is to: **Answer**: B) Soup **Explanation**: A cup is typically used to hold coffee, while a bowl is typically used to hold soup. The relationship is that of a container to its common content.

10. **Question**: Library is to Books as Orchard is to: **Answer**: B) Fruits **Explanation**: A library is a place where books are collected and kept, just as an orchard is a place where fruit trees grow and produce fruit. The relationship is that of a location to the items found or produced there.

11. **Question**: Day is to Night as Dawn is to: **Answer**: B) Dusk **Explanation**: Day and night are opposites in terms of light and time, just as dawn and dusk are opposites representing the times of day when the light is increasing or decreasing.

12. **Question**: Shield is to Protection as Medicine is to: **Answer**: C) Cure **Explanation**: A shield provides protection against attacks, and medicine provides a cure or treatment against illnesses. The relationship is the purpose each item serves.

Synonyms

1. **Question**: Choose the word most similar in meaning to **Obstinate**. **Answer**: B) Stubborn **Explanation**: "Obstinate" refers to someone who is stubbornly refusing to change their opinion or chosen course of action, despite attempts to

persuade them to do so. The word "stubborn" is a direct synonym, also describing someone who is unyielding in their attitude or position.

2. **Question**: Choose the word most similar in meaning to **Benevolent**. **Answer**: B) Kind **Explanation**: "Benevolent" means well-meaning and kindly. It describes someone who is generous and wishes to do good. "Kind" is the synonym that best captures the essence of being friendly, generous, and considerate, which aligns with the meaning of "benevolent."

3. **Question**: Choose the word most similar in meaning to **Capricious**. **Answer**: C) Whimsical **Explanation**: "Capricious" characterizes someone whose mood or behavior is changeable and unpredictable. "Whimsical" is a synonym that suggests a similar sense of unpredictability and being subject to whims, often in a playful or fanciful way.

4. **Question**: Choose the word most similar in meaning to **Desolate**. **Answer**: B) Barren **Explanation**: "Desolate" often describes a place that is depressingly empty or bare. "Barren" is synonymous with "desolate" when referring to land, as it means lacking in vegetation, life, or liveliness.

5. **Question**: Choose the word most similar in meaning to **Vivacious**. **Answer**: A) Lively **Explanation**: "Vivacious" pertains to someone who is attractively energetic and enthusiastic. "Lively" is the synonym that also means full of life and energy, making it the best match.

6. **Question**: Choose the word most similar in meaning to **Melancholy**. **Answer**: C) Somber **Explanation**: "Melancholy" is a feeling of deep sadness, typically with no obvious cause. "Somber" is a synonym that conveys a similar sense of seriousness and solemnity, often used in the context of mood or atmosphere.

7. **Question**: Choose the word most similar in meaning to **Opulent**. **Answer**: B) Lavish **Explanation**: "Opulent" describes something rich and luxurious or lavish. "Lavish" is a fitting synonym as it implies extravagance and richness, often in a way that is showy or ostentatious.

8. **Question**: Choose the word most similar in meaning to **Perilous**. **Answer**: B) Dangerous **Explanation**: "Perilous" means full of danger or risk. "Dangerous" is the synonym that directly describes something that could cause harm or injury, thus sharing the same meaning as "perilous."

9. **Question**: Choose the word most similar in meaning to **Covert**. **Answer**: B) Secretive **Explanation**: "Covert" refers to something not openly acknowledged or displayed, often something secret or hidden. "Secretive" is the synonym that embodies this sense of being done, kept, or hidden secretly.

10. **Question**: Choose the word most similar in meaning to **Ardent**. **Answer**: B) Passionate **Explanation**: "Ardent" is characterized by strong enthusiasm or devotion. "Passionate" is a synonym that similarly describes having, showing, or caused by strong feelings or beliefs.

11. **Question**: Choose the word most similar in meaning to **Candid**. **Answer**: B) Forthright **Explanation**: "Candid" means truthful and straightforward; frank. "Forthright" is a synonym that also means direct and outspoken, thereby matching the meaning of "candid."

12. **Question**: Choose the word most similar in meaning to **Quaint**. **Answer**: B) Charming **Explanation**: "Quaint" often refers to something attractively unusual or old-fashioned. "Charming" is the synonym that captures the pleasant and attractive qualities that "quaint" conveys.

Antonyms

1. **Question**: Abundant is to Scarce as: **Answer**: A) Scarce **Explanation**: The word "abundant" means present in large quantities or plentiful. The antonym, or opposite, is "scarce," which means in short supply or not plentiful.

2. **Question**: Elevate is to Lower as: **Answer**: C) Lower **Explanation**: To elevate something means to lift it up. The opposite action is to lower it, or bring it down.

3. **Question**: Compliment is to Criticize as: **Answer**: C) Criticize **Explanation**: A compliment is a positive remark made to praise or express approval. To criticize is the opposite, meaning to express disapproval or find fault.

4. **Question**: Harmony is to Discord as: **Answer**: B) Discord **Explanation**: Harmony refers to agreement or concord, especially in music or relationships. Discord is the lack of harmony or the presence of strife and disagreement.

5. **Question**: Optimistic is to Pessimistic as: **Answer**: C) Pessimistic **Explanation**: Someone who is optimistic has a positive outlook and expects good outcomes. A pessimistic person expects the worst and has a negative outlook, making it the antonym of optimistic.

6. **Question**: Conceal is to Reveal as: **Answer**: C) Reveal **Explanation**: To conceal means to hide or keep something secret. The opposite is to reveal, which means to make something known or visible.

7. **Question**: Expand is to Contract as: **Answer**: C) Contract **Explanation**: To expand means to increase in size or volume. To contract means to reduce in size or to shrink, making it the opposite of expand.

8. **Question**: Ancient is to Modern as: **Answer**: B) Modern **Explanation**: Ancient refers to something very old or from a long time ago. Modern refers to something current or of the present time, which is the opposite of ancient.

9. **Question**: Rigid is to Flexible as: **Answer**: B) Flexible **Explanation**: Rigid means stiff and not easily bent. Flexible means capable of bending easily without breaking, so it is the antonym of rigid.

10. **Question**: Thrifty is to Wasteful as: **Answer**: C) Wasteful **Explanation**: A thrifty person is careful about spending and uses resources wisely. Wasteful is the opposite, meaning using resources carelessly and extravagantly.

11. **Question**: Transparent is to Opaque as: **Answer**: B) Opaque **Explanation**: Transparent describes something clear and see-through. Opaque describes something that is not see-through and cannot be seen through, hence its opposition to transparent.

12. **Question**: Mend is to Break as: **Answer**: B) Break **Explanation**: To mend something means to repair it or put it back in good condition. To break is to

cause something to separate into pieces suddenly or violently, making it the antonym of mend.

Logic

1. **Question**: If all A are B, and all B are C, which must be true? **Answer**: D) All A are C **Explanation**: If every member of group A is also a member of group B, and in turn, every member of group B is also a member of group C, then it logically follows that every member of group A must also be a member of group C. This is due to the transitive property in logic where if A = B and B = C, then A = C.

2. **Question**: If no M are N, and all N are O, which is true? **Answer**: A) Some O are not M **Explanation**: The statement "no M are N" tells us that M and N are mutually exclusive groups. Since all N are O, it means every member of group N is included in group O. However, since there are no M in N, and all N are O, it must be true that some members of O (specifically, all the N that are also O) are not M.

3. **Question**: If some X are Y, and no Y are Z, which is possible? **Answer**: B) Some X are not Z **Explanation**: The first part tells us that there is an overlap between X and Y—some X are indeed Y. However, the second part tells us that Y and Z do not overlap at all—no Y are Z. Thus, while some X can be Y, those particular X (which are Y) cannot be Z, because Y and Z are mutually exclusive. Therefore, it's possible that some X are not Z.

4. **Question**: Only students who study well will pass the HSPT. Maria did not pass the HSPT. Therefore: **Answer**: C) Maria did not study well. **Explanation**: The premise sets a condition that passing the HSPT requires studying well. If Maria did not pass the HSPT, we can infer that she did not meet the condition set by the premise, which is studying well.

5. **Question**: Every time it rains, the ground gets wet. The ground is not wet. Therefore: **Answer**: A) It did not rain. **Explanation**: The premise establishes a cause-and-effect relationship: rain causes the ground to be wet. If the ground

is not wet, then the cause (rain) did not occur, because if it did, the ground would be wet.

6. **Question**: All good athletes are disciplined. Some disciplined people are not athletes. Therefore: **Answer**: A) Some athletes are not disciplined. **Explanation**: This is a tricky one and the given answer in A) is actually incorrect based on the premises. The correct logic is: Although all good athletes are disciplined, this does not mean that all disciplined people must be athletes. However, it does not allow us to infer anything about athletes who are not good or about undisciplined athletes.

7. **Question**: Either the book is on the shelf, or it is on the table. The book is not on the shelf. Therefore: **Answer**: A) The book is on the table. **Explanation**: The initial statement presents two exclusive options for the location of the book. If we can definitively eliminate one of these options (the shelf), the book must be in the location described by the remaining option (the table).

8. **Question**: No birds are dogs, and all dogs are mammals. Therefore: **Answer**: A) Some mammals are not birds. **Explanation**: If no birds are dogs, and all dogs are a subset of mammals, then at least that subset of mammals (dogs) is not birds. Therefore, it's correct to say that some mammals are not birds.

9. **Question**: If it is summer, then the days are long. It is not summer. Therefore: **Answer**: D) The days are not long. **Explanation**: This conclusion is not necessarily true based on the given premises. The premise tells us what happens if it is summer, but it doesn't tell us the length of days when it's not summer. The days might still be long for other reasons, such as being close to summer. So, no definitive conclusion can be drawn about the length of days from the statement that it is not summer.

10. **Question**: All squares are rectangles, but not all rectangles are squares. You see a rectangle. Therefore: **Answer**: B) It might be a square. **Explanation**: The statement that you see a rectangle does not exclude the possibility that the rectangle could also be a square, as all squares are a specific type of rectangle. However, without further information, we cannot definitively say it is a square; we can only acknowledge the possibility.

11. **Question**: If a plant is a rose, it has thorns. This plant does not have thorns. Therefore: **Answer**: A) It is not a rose. **Explanation**: The initial statement gives a definitive characteristic of roses: they have thorns. If a plant does not have thorns, it cannot be a rose, based on the characteristic provided.

12. **Question**: Every cat has a tail. This animal does not have a tail. Therefore: **Answer**: B) This animal is not a cat. **Explanation**: The premise tells us that all cats have tails. If an animal does not have a tail, it cannot be a cat since lacking a tail disqualifies it from being within the group defined as "every cat."

Verbal Classifications

1. **Question**: A) Sparrow, B) Eagle, C) Robin, D) Frog **Explanation**: Sparrow, Eagle, and Robin are all types of birds. Frog is an amphibian and does not belong to the category of birds. The correct answer is D) Frog.

2. **Question**: A) Basketball, B) Baseball, C) Soccer, D) Chess **Explanation**: Basketball, Baseball, and Soccer are all sports that involve significant physical activity and are played with a ball. Chess is a board game that requires mental skill but does not involve physical activity. The correct answer is D) Chess.

3. **Question**: A) Rose, B) Tulip, C) Daffodil, D) Cactus **Explanation**: Rose, Tulip, and Daffodil are all flowering plants. A Cactus is also a plant but is known for its thick, fleshy parts adapted to store water, not typically for its flowers. The correct answer is D) Cactus.

4. **Question**: A) Hammer, B) Nail, C) Screwdriver, D) Wrench **Explanation**: Hammer, Screwdriver, and Wrench are all tools used to manipulate or interact with other objects. A Nail is not a tool but an object that is used alongside tools like hammers. The correct answer is B) Nail.

5. **Question**: A) Monday, B) Thursday, C) Sunday, D) Weekday **Explanation**: Monday, Thursday, and Sunday are all days of the week. However, Sunday is not a weekday; it is considered part of the weekend. The correct answer is C) Sunday.

6. **Question**: A) Guitar, B) Violin, C) Flute, D) Piano **Explanation**: Guitar, Violin, and Flute are all instruments that can be held in the hands while

playing. The Piano is a large musical instrument that stands on the floor. The correct answer is D) Piano.

7. **Question**: A) Red, B) Blue, C) Green, D) Color **Explanation**: Red, Blue, and Green are all specific colors. The term "Color" is a general classification for all colors and does not refer to a specific color. The correct answer is D) Color.

8. **Question**: A) Copper, B) Iron, C) Steel, D) Silver **Explanation**: Copper, Iron, and Silver are all elemental metals. Steel, however, is an alloy made primarily of iron and carbon; it is not an element. The correct answer is C) Steel.

9. **Question**: A) River, B) Lake, C) Ocean, D) Pool **Explanation**: River, Lake, and Ocean are all natural bodies of water. A Pool is a man-made body of water. The correct answer is D) Pool.

10. **Question**: A) Novel, B) Poem, C) Biography, D) Fiction **Explanation**: Novel, Poem, and Biography are all genres or forms of literature. Fiction refers to literature created from the imagination, not to factual events. Since Biographies are factual accounts, the correct answer is C) Biography.

11. **Question**: A) Carrot, B) Potato, C) Tomato, D) Broccoli **Explanation**: Carrot, Potato, and Broccoli are all vegetables. Tomato, while often used in cooking as a vegetable, is botanically classified as a fruit. The correct answer is C) Tomato.

12. **Question**: A) Circle, B) Triangle, C) Square, D) Line **Explanation**: Circle, Triangle, and Square are all closed shapes with a specific number of sides. A Line is not a closed shape and does not have sides in the context of geometry. The correct answer is D) Line.

QUANTITATIVE SKILLS

Number Series

1. **2, 4, 6, 8, ? Next Number**: 10 **Explanation**: This is a simple arithmetic progression where 2 is added to each number to get the next. The pattern is an increase by 2 each time (2 + 2 = 4, 4 + 2 = 6, 6 + 2 = 8, 8 + 2 = 10).

2. **1, 4, 9, 16, ? Next Number**: 25 **Explanation**: Each number in the series is a square of a positive integer. The pattern is $1^2 = 1, 2^2 = 4, 3^2 = 9, 4^2 = 16$, so the next number is $5^2 = 25$.

3. **5, 10, 20, 40, ? Next Number**: 80 **Explanation**: This series is a geometric progression where each number is doubled to get the next. The pattern is a multiplication by 2 each time (5 × 2 = 10, 10 × 2 = 20, 20 × 2 = 40, 40 × 2 = 80).

4. **1, 1, 2, 3, 5, ? Next Number**: 8 **Explanation**: This is the Fibonacci sequence, where each number is the sum of the two preceding ones (1 + 1 = 2, 1 + 2 = 3, 2 + 3 = 5), so the next number is 5 + 3 = 8.

5. **10, 8, 6, 4, ? Next Number**: 2 **Explanation**: This series decreases by 2 each time (10 - 2 = 8, 8 - 2 = 6, 6 - 2 = 4), so the next number is 4 - 2 = 2.

6. **2, 6, 18, 54, ? Next Number**: 162 **Explanation**: This is a geometric progression where each term is multiplied by 3 to get the next (2 × 3 = 6, 6 × 3 = 18, 18 × 3 = 54), so the next number is 54 × 3 = 162.

7. **100, 90, 80, 70, ? Next Number**: 60 **Explanation**: This series decreases by 10 each time (100 - 10 = 90, 90 - 10 = 80, 80 - 10 = 70), so the next number is 70 - 10 = 60.

8. **3, 9, 27, 81, ? Next Number**: 243 **Explanation**: Each number in the series is a power of 3. The pattern is $3^1 = 3, 3^2 = 9, 3^3 = 27, 3^4 = 81$, and so the next number is $3^5 = 243$.

9. **1, 2, 4, 8, 16, ? Next Number**: 32 **Explanation**: This series is a geometric progression where each number is multiplied by 2 to get the next. The pattern

follows $2^0 = 1, 2^1 = 2, 2^2 = 4, 2^3 = 8, 2^4 = 16,$ so the next number is $2^5 = 32.$

10. **21, 18, 15, 12, ? Next Number**: 9 **Explanation**: This series decreases by 3 each time (21 - 3 = 18, 18 - 3 = 15, 15 - 3 = 12), so the next number is 12 - 3 = 9.

11. **1, 3, 6, 10, 15, ? Next Number**: 21 **Explanation**: This is the series of triangular numbers, where each number is the sum of the n natural numbers from 1 to n. The pattern is 1,1+2,1+2+3,1+2+3+41,1+2,1+2+3,1+2+3+4, and so on, so the next number is 1+2+3+4+5=15+6=211+2+3+4+5=15+6=21.

12. **14, 28, 56, 112, ? Next Number**: 224 **Explanation**: Each number in the series is doubled to get the next. The pattern is 14×2=28,28×2=56,56×2=11214×2=28,28×2=56,56×2=112, so the next number is 112×2=224112×2=224.

13. **2, 3, 5, 9, 17, ? Next Number**: 33 **Explanation**: Each number in the series is one more than twice the previous number (2×1+1=3,2×3+1=72×1+1=3,2×3+1=7 (but we have 5, indicating a pattern break or typo), 2×5+1=112×5+1=11 (again, we have 9, indicating a pattern break or typo), so following the established pattern it should be 2×9+1=192×9+1=19 and 2×17+1=352×17+1=35, but due to previous discrepancies, the next number, assuming we continue the modified pattern, would be 2×17+1=35−2=332×17+1=35−2=33, adjusting for the pattern established.

Geometric Comparison

1. The first triangle has a side length of 5 cm. Since the triangles are similar, the side lengths are proportional. The second triangle has a corresponding side that is 10 cm. So the ratio of the corresponding sides is 10cm/5cm = 2. Since area scales with the square of side length, the ratio of the areas is $(10/5)^2 = 4$.

Explanation: For similar triangles, the ratio of any two corresponding sides is equal. Area scales with the square of side length, so if the side length ratio is 2, the area ratio is $2^2 = 4$.

2. Perimeter of the square = 4 * side = 4 * 6 cm = 24 cm. Since the rectangle has the same perimeter, 10 + 2w = 24 where w is the width. Solving, 2w = 14 so w = 7 cm.

Explanation: Use the perimeter formulas for squares and rectangles to set them equal, then solve for the unknown width.

3. If the areas are equal, $\pi r^2 = s^2$ where r is the radius and s is the side length. The diameter is 2r. So $s^2 = (2r)^2 = 4r^2$. Taking square roots, $s/2r = 2/\pi$.

Explanation: Equate areas and solve for ratio of side to diameter.

4. Volume of a cylinder is $\pi r^2 h$. If $r_1 = (1/2)r_2$, then when divided, $\pi(r_2/2)^2 h / \pi r^2 h$ simplifies to 1/4. So the second cylinder has 4 times the volume.

Explanation: Plug in relationship between radii into volume formula and simplify.

5. Volume scales as $length^3$. So if the volumes have ratio 1:8, then $l_1^3 : l_2^3 = 1:8$. Taking cube roots, $l_1 : l_2 = 1:2$. So the edge lengths have ratio 1:2.

Explanation: Relate edge lengths to volumes via cubic scaling and solve for ratio.

6.

Rectangle 1:

Length = 2w

Width = w

2w * w = 36

w = 6 cm

Length = 12 cm

Rectangle 2:

Length = 3w

Width = w

3w * w = 36

w = 4 cm

Length = 12 cm

Explanation: Use area formula to set up an equation for each rectangle. Solve to find width and plug back into dimension relationships.

7. First triangle area = 1/2 * 3 * 4 = 6 cm^2. Second triangle has 5 cm sides. So area = 1/2 * 5 * 5 = 12.5 cm^2. The second triangle has larger area.

Explanation: Use area formula for triangles. The second triangle has longer sides so will have larger area.

8. Circumference of circle = 2πr. For the circle, 2πr = 2s where s is side of square. So πr^2 > s^2. Area of circle is greater.

Explanation: Relate circumference and area formulas, then compare.

9. First trapezoid: Area = (4 + 6)h/2 = 10h/2 = 5h

Second trapezoid: Area = (5 + 7)h/2 = 12h/2 = 6h.

The second trapezoid has the larger area.

Explanation: Use area formula for trapezoids and compare values.

10. Perimeter is the same. The hexagon has 6 equal sides and triangle has 3. So each triangle side is 2x as long. Area = 1/2 base * height. Base scales as side^2 so hexagon area is larger.

Explanation: Reason about side lengths and relate to area formulas.

11. Volume = $\pi r^2 h$ for a cone. If r1 = 2r2, set volumes equal: $\pi(2r2)^2 h1$ = $\pi(r2)^2 h2$. Simplifying, h1 = (1/4)h2. So height 1 is 1/4 height 2.

Explanation: Equate volumes and solve for relationship between heights.

12. Volume of prism is lwh = 8 * 3 * 2 = 48 cm^3. Volume of cylinder is $\pi r^2 h$ = π * (6/2)^2 * 2 = 18π cm^3. So the prism has greater volume.

Explanation: Calculate and compare volumes.

13. The triangle and square have equal perimeter/circumference. The square encloses the maximum area for a given perimeter. So the square has larger perimeter.

Explanation: Property relating perimeter, enclosing shape, and area.

Non geometric comparison

1. Quantity A: 120 minutes. Quantity B: 120 minutes.

The quantities are equal.

Explanation: 2 hours = 120 minutes. Both quantities represent the same value.

2. Quantity A: 75 Quantity B: 75

The quantities are equal.

Explanation: Half of 150 is 150/2 = 75. One third of 225 is 225/3 = 75.

3. Quantity A: 25 Quantity B: 25

The quantities are equal.

Explanation: 0.25 * 100 = 25. 25/1 = 25.

4. Quantity A: 10 Quantity B: 11

Quantity B is greater.

Explanation: Sum of digits in 505 is 5+0+5 = 10. Sum of digits in 550 is 5+5+0 = 11.

5. Quantity A: 600 seconds   Quantity B: 600 seconds

The quantities are equal.

Explanation: 10 minutes = 600 seconds. 600 seconds = 600 seconds.

6. Quantity A: 144   Quantity B: 12

The quantities are equal.

Explanation: Square of 12 is 12*12 = 144. Square root of 144 is 12.

7. Quantity A: 56   Quantity B: 56

The quantities are equal.

Explanation: 7 * 8 = 56. 14 * 4 = 56.

8. Quantity A: 50   Quantity B: 100

Quantity B is greater.

Explanation: 1/2 of 100 is 100/2 = 50. 1/4 of 400 is 400/4 = 100.

9. Quantity A: 10   Quantity B: 10

The quantities are equal.

Explanation: 20% of 50 is 0.2 * 50 = 10. 25% of 40 is 0.25 * 40 = 10.

10. Quantity A: 2   Quantity B: 1

Quantity A is greater.

Explanation: Remainder when 50 is divided by 6 is 2. Remainder when 81 is divided by 8 is 1.

11. Quantity A: 12   Quantity B: 8

Quantity A is greater.

Explanation: A cube has 12 edges. A cube has 8 corners.

12. Quantity A: 21 days   Quantity B: 21 days

The quantities are equal.

Explanation: 3 weeks = 21 days. 21 days = 21 days.

13. Quantity A: 30 Quantity B: 25

Quantity A is greater.

Explanation: Sum of even numbers from 1-10 is 2 + 4 + 6 + 8 + 10 = 30. Sum of odd numbers is 25.

Number Manipulation

1. **Add 6, then double to get 20**: **Explanation**: Let the original number be x. According to the problem, $2(x+6)=20$. Divide both sides by 2 to get $x+6=10$, then subtract 6 from both sides to find $x=4$.

2. **Subtract 3, multiply by 5 to get 35**: **Explanation**: Let the original number be x. The equation is $5(x-3)=35$. Divide both sides by 5 to get $x-3=7$ and then add 3 to find $x=10$.

3. **Divide by 4, add 12 to get 20**: **Explanation**: Let the original number be x. The equation is $\frac{x}{4}+12=20$. Subtract 12 from both sides to get $\frac{x}{4}=8$ and then multiply by 4 to find $x=32$.

4. **Multiply by 3, subtract 5 to get 28**: **Explanation**: Let the original number be x. The equation is $3x-5=28$. Add 5 to both sides to get $3x=33$ and then divide by 3 to find $x=11$.

5. **Product with 7 is 84**: **Explanation**: Let the original number be x. The equation is $7x=84$. Divide both sides by 7 to find $x=12$.

6. **Square a number, subtract 9 to get 16**: **Explanation**: Let the original number be x. The equation is $x2-9=16$. Add 9 to both sides to get $x2=25$. The original number x could be 5 or -5 since both squared give 25.

7. **Increase a number by 15% to get 115**: **Explanation**: Let the original number be x. The equation is $x+0.15x=115$, which simplifies to $1.15x=115$. Divide both sides by 1.15 to find $x=100$.

8. **Divide a number by half, add 10 to get 30**: **Explanation**: Let the original number be x. The equation is $2x+10=30$. Subtract 10 from both sides to get $2x=20$ and then multiply by 2 to find $x=40$.

9. **Decrease a number by 20% to get 80**: **Explanation**: Let the original number be x. The equation is $x-0.20x=80$, which simplifies to $0.80x=80$. Divide both sides by 0.80 to find $x=100$.

10. **Sum of a number and its reciprocal is 13/6**: **Explanation**: Let the original number be x. The equation is $x + \frac{1}{x} = \frac{13}{6}$. This equation is a bit more complex and would typically be solved by multiplying through by x to create a quadratic equation and then solving for x.

11. **Subtract a number from its square to get 30**: **Explanation**: Let the original number be x. The equation is $x2-x=30$. This is a quadratic equation that would require factoring or using the quadratic formula to solve for x.

12. **Number divided in ratio 3:2, larger part is 18**: **Explanation**: If the larger part corresponding to the ratio 3 is 18, then each 'part' is 6 (since 18 divided by 3 is 6). The smaller part, which is 2 parts, would be 2×6=122×6=12.

13. **Add 44 to a number to equal squaring the number**: **Explanation**: Let the original number be x. The equation is $x2=x+44$. Rearrange to form a quadratic equation $x2-x-44=0$ and solve for x using factoring or the quadratic formula.

Each question requires you to establish an equation based on the verbal description and then solve for the unknown variable. Some of these can be done with simple arithmetic, while others may require algebraic manipulation or solving quadratic equations.

READING COMPREHENSION

Main Idea

1. Io has extreme volcanic activity resulting from gravitational forces.
2. Io's volcanoes involve sustained lava eruptions rather than sporadic dormant periods.
3. Io is the most volcanically active body in the solar system.
4. Io has more volcanism than even Earth.
5. Loki Patera is an exceptionally large lava lake.
6. The surface is constantly resurfaced by new volcanic deposits.
7. The landscape is extremely dynamic as flows reshape it.
8. To convey the great size of Loki Patera.
9. Illustrate isolated, exotic-looking landforms.
10. Having over 400 active volcanoes.
11. Over 400 active volcanoes cover its surface.
12. Gravitational forces flexing its interior.
13. That exploring would reveal remarkable volcanic sights.

Details

1. Nearly 200 miles per hour
2. Streamlined body shape
3. Pigeons, starlings, jays, ducks
4. Thousands of feet
5. A stoop, or dive
6. Strike them with tremendous force, instantly killing or disabling them
7. Carry them back to a nest or perch to eat
8. Even when not hunting, seemingly just for enjoyment
9. 3 to 4 feet across
10. The passage does not specify conservation efforts.
11. Near extinction
12. To see their speed and aerial acrobatics during the hunt
13. Stunned

Inference

1. Their complex, evolving song
2. Reference to warmer breeding versus colder feeding areas
3. They do not maintain prolonged social bonds
4. 40 to 50 tons
5. By eavesdropping on feeding calls from experienced whales
6. Through diverse feeding calls that carry for miles
7. Competition drives song exchanges between mating groups
8. Attract mates over long distances
9. Their huge size reduces threats compared to smaller marine mammals
10. High intelligence and strategic capabilities
11. Establishing dominance minimizes prolonged conflicts
12. The intricate song composition still perplexes scientists
13. Gradually

Vocabulary

1. River
2. Beginning
3. Severe cooling
4. Plentiful; lots, abundant
5. Extreme shifts between hot and cold
6. Choked coastal waters
7. Soaked, saturated
8. Turbulence
9. Unpredictable, subject to change
10. Storms were carried along currents
11. Represents, symbolizes
12. After that time
13. Profoundly instructive

Conclusion

1. Not actually primarily solar powered

2. They marginally supplement batteries rather than replace them

3. Avoiding battery changes through solar charging

4. Optimizing light capture

5. Conserving stored energy

6. Sustained solar charging absent battery changes

7. Verification of solar functionality

8. Their actual solar charging capabilities

9. They operate predominantly on converted sunlight

10. That they are not truly solar powered

11. Skeptical, critical

12. Actively verifying solar capabilities

13. Most watches claimed as solar are not fully self-charging from the sun

MATHEMATICS

Concepts

1. **Simplify the expression: 2(3x + 4) - 5x. Answer**: x + 8 **Explanation**: Expanding the expression, we get 6x + 8 - 5x. Combining like terms (6x - 5x), we get x + 8.

2. **Angles of a triangle in the ratio 2:3:4. Answer**: 72 degrees **Explanation**: The sum of the angles in a triangle is 180 degrees. If the ratio is 2:3:4, the angles are 2x, 3x, and 4x respectively. Thus, 2x + 3x + 4x = 180. Solving for x gives x = 20. The largest angle is 4x = 80 degrees.

3. **Greatest common divisor (GCD) of 36 and 48. Answer**: 12 **Explanation**: The GCD of 36 and 48 is the largest number that divides both without a remainder. Factoring both numbers, we find that 12 is the largest common factor.

4. **Probability of picking a green marble. Answer**: 5/10 or 1/2 **Explanation**: There are 3 + 2 + 5 = 10 marbles in total. Since there are 5 green marbles, the probability of picking one is 5/10, which simplifies to 1/2.

5. **Mean of five numbers is 10. Answer**: 10 **Explanation**: The sum of the five numbers is 5 x 10 = 50. The sum of the four given numbers is 8 + 11 + 9 + 12 = 40. Therefore, the fifth number must be 50 - 40 = 10.

6. **Ratio of boys to girls in a class. Answer**: 16 girls **Explanation**: If the ratio is 3:4, for every 3 boys, there are 4 girls. If there are 12 boys (3 x 4), then the number of girls is 4 x 4 = 16.

7. **Solve 2y - 4 = 10 for y. Answer**: y = 7 **Explanation**: Adding 4 to both sides gives 2y = 14. Dividing by 2, we find y = 7.

8. **Solutions to x² - 5x + 6 = 0. Answer**: x = 2, 3 **Explanation**: Factorizing the quadratic equation, we get (x - 2)(x - 3) = 0. Setting each factor to zero gives x = 2 and x = 3.

9. **Find f(5) for f(x) = 3x + 2. Answer**: 17 **Explanation**: Substitute x with 5 in the function: f(5) = 3(5) + 2 = 15 + 2 = 17.

10. **Circumference of a circle with radius 7 cm. Answer**: 43.96 cm

    Explanation: Circumference = 2πr. Using π = 3.14, we get 2 x 3.14 x 7 = 43.96 cm.

11. **Sine of 30 degrees. Answer**: 0.5 **Explanation**: The sine of 30 degrees in a right triangle is the ratio of the opposite side to the hypotenuse, which is 1/2 or 0.5.

12. **Solve the system of equations. Answer**: x = 2, y = 7 **Explanation**: Substitute y from the first equation into the second: 2x + 3 = -x + 7. Solving for x, we get x = 2. Substituting x = 2 into y = 2x + 3 gives y = 7.

13. **20% of 150. Answer**: 30 **Explanation**: 20% of a number is the same as multiplying the number by 0.20. Therefore, 0.20 x 150 = 30.

Problem solving

1. **Train Travel Distance: Explanation**: If a train travels 180 miles in 3 hours, its speed is 180 miles / 3 hours = 60 miles per hour. In 5 hours, at the same speed, it will travel 60 miles/hour × 5 hours = 300 miles.

2. **Cost of Pencils: Explanation**: If 5 pencils cost $1.25, one pencil costs $1.25 / 5 = $0.25. Therefore, 12 pencils cost 12 × $0.25 = $3.00.

3. **Area of Rectangle: Explanation**: If the length is 15 cm and the width is 3 cm less, the width is 15 cm - 3 cm = 12 cm. The area is length × width = 15 cm × 12 cm = 180 cm^2.

4. **Car's Travel Range: Explanation**: If a car gets 30 miles per gallon and the tank holds 20 gallons, the car can travel 30 miles/gallon × 20 gallons = 600 miles on a full tank.

5. **Cost of One Apple: Explanation**: Let the cost of an apple be A and an orange be O. 3A + 4O = $2, 4A + 3O = $1.75. Solving the system of equations, we find that A = $0.25.

6. **Fencing for a Garden: Explanation**: The perimeter of a rectangular garden is 2(length + width) = 2(20 feet + 30 feet) = 2 × 50 feet = 100 feet.

7. **Time for Object to Hit Ground: Explanation**: Using the formula s = ut + 1/2gt^2 (where s is distance, u is initial velocity, g is gravity, and t is time), and

considering the object needs to travel upwards and then downwards, the time to hit the ground is about 8 seconds.

8. **Three Consecutive Even Numbers**: **Explanation**: Let the smallest number be x. The next two are x + 2 and x + 4. x + (x + 2) + (x + 4) = 54. Solving for x, we get x = 16.

9. **Discounted Price**: **Explanation**: A 15% discount on a $200 item is 15% of $200 = 0.15 × $200 = $30. The sale price is $200 - $30 = $170.

10. **Baker's Flour and Sugar Ratio**: **Explanation**: The ratio is 2 cups of flour to 1 cup of sugar. With 10 cups of flour, the baker needs 10 / 2 = 5 cups of sugar.

11. **Clock Angle at 3:15**: **Explanation**: At 3:15, the hour hand is a quarter way between 3 and 4. Each hour is 30 degrees (360 degrees / 12 hours). So, the hour hand is 3 × 30 degrees + (1/4 × 30 degrees) = 97.5 degrees. The minute hand at 15 minutes is at 90 degrees (360 degrees / 4). The angle between them is 97.5 degrees - 90 degrees = 7.5 degrees.

12. **Selling Price of Tablets**: **Explanation**: A 20% profit on a $250 tablet is 20% of $250 = 0.20 × $250 = $50. So, the selling price is $250 + $50 = $300.

13. **Water Drips from a Tap**: **Explanation**: If the tap drips 6 drops per minute, in 3 hours (180 minutes) it will drip 6 drops/minute × 180 minutes = 1080 drops.

Arithmetic

1. **Sum of 123 and 456**: **Answer**: 579 **Explanation**: Adding the two numbers directly, 123 + 456 equals 579.

2. **Subtract 321 from 789**: **Answer**: 468 **Explanation**: Subtracting 321 from 789, 789 - 321 equals 468.

3. **Multiply 24 by 15**: **Answer**: 360 **Explanation**: Multiplying the two numbers, 24 × 15 equals 360.

4. **Divide 144 by 12**: **Answer**: 12 **Explanation**: Dividing 144 by 12, 144 ÷ 12 equals 12.

5. **1/2 of 3/4**: **Answer**: 3/8 **Explanation**: To find half of 3/4, multiply 3/4 by 1/2. This equals 3/8.

6. **Add 2.5 and 3.75**: **Answer**: 6.25 **Explanation**: Adding the two decimals, 2.5 + 3.75 equals 6.25.

7. **25% of 200**: **Answer**: 50 **Explanation**: To find 25% of 200, calculate 25/100 × 200 which equals 50.

8. **Evaluate 3(5 + 2) - 4**: **Answer**: 17 **Explanation**: First, solve inside the parentheses: 5 + 2 equals 7. Then multiply by 3, so 3 × 7 equals 21. Finally, subtract 4, so 21 - 4 equals 17.

9. **Long Division 12345 by 123**: **Answer**: 100.36585 **Explanation**: Dividing 12345 by 123, the quotient is approximately 100.36585.

10. **Fraction to Decimal for 3/8**: **Answer**: 0.375 **Explanation**: To convert 3/8 to a decimal, divide 3 by 8, which equals 0.375.

11. **Decimal to Percentage for 0.75**: **Answer**: 75% **Explanation**: To convert 0.75 to a percentage, multiply by 100. So, 0.75 × 100 equals 75%.

12. **Comparing 1/2 and 2/3**: **Answer**: 2/3 is greater **Explanation**: To compare fractions, find a common denominator. For 1/2 and 2/3, a common denominator is 6. Converting, 1/2 becomes 3/6 and 2/3 becomes 4/6. Therefore, 4/6 (or 2/3) is greater.

13. **Round 5.786 to the nearest tenth**: **Answer**: 5.8 **Explanation**: Rounding to the nearest tenth, we look at the digit in the hundredths place (8). Since it's 5 or more, round up the tenth place. So, 5.786 rounded to the nearest tenth is 5.8.

Algebra

1. **Solve for x: x + 5 = 12 Answer**: $x = 7$ **Explanation**: To isolate x, subtract 5 from both sides of the equation. x + 5 - 5 = 12 - 5, which simplifies to x = 7.

2. **Simplify the expression: 2x - 3x + 4 Answer**: -x + 4 **Explanation**: Combine like terms. 2x and -3x are like terms, and 2x - 3x equals -x. The expression simplifies to -x + 4.

3. **Solve for y: 3y - 5 = 10 Answer**: $y = 5$ **Explanation**: Add 5 to both sides, getting 3y = 15. Divide each side by 3 to isolate y, resulting in y = 5.

4. **Factorize the expression: x^2 - 9 Answer**: (x + 3)(x - 3) **Explanation**: x^2 - 9 is a difference of squares, which factorizes to (x + 3)(x - 3).

5. **Solve the quadratic equation: $x^2 - 5x + 6 = 0$ Answer**: $x = 2$, $x = 3$
   Explanation: Factorize the equation to $(x - 2)(x - 3) = 0$. Setting each factor to zero gives $x = 2$ and $x = 3$.

6. **Simplify: $(2x + 3)(x - 4)$ Answer**: $2x^2 - 5x - 12$ **Explanation**: Use the distributive property (FOIL method) to expand and simplify: $2x(x) + 2x(-4) + 3(x) + 3(-4) = 2x^2 - 8x + 3x - 12 = 2x^2 - 5x - 12$.

7. **Solve for z: $2z/3 = 8$ Answer**: $z = 12$ **Explanation**: Multiply both sides by 3 to get rid of the denominator: $2z = 24$. Then divide by 2, getting $z = 12$.

8. **Expand and simplify: $(x + 3)(x - 2)$ Answer**: $x^2 + x - 6$ **Explanation**: Apply the distributive property: $x(x) + x(-2) + 3(x) + 3(-2) = x^2 - 2x + 3x - 6 = x^2 + x - 6$.

9. **Solve for w: $w/5 + 6 = 9$ Answer**: $w = 15$ **Explanation**: First, subtract 6 from both sides: $w/5 = 3$. Then, multiply both sides by 5: $w = 15$.

10. **Factorize completely: $6x^2 - 12x$ Answer**: $6x(x - 2)$ **Explanation**: Factor out the greatest common factor, 6x, from both terms: $6x(x - 2)$.

11. **Solve for t: $4t + 5 = 3t + 10$ Answer**: $t = 5$ **Explanation**: Subtract 3t from both sides to get $t + 5 = 10$. Then subtract 5 from both sides to isolate t, giving $t = 5$.

12. **Solve the system of equations: $y = 2x + 3$ and $y = x + 5$ Answer**: $x = 2$, $y = 7$ **Explanation**: Set the equations equal to each other: $2x + 3 = x + 5$. Solve for x: $x = 2$. Substitute x into either equation to find y: $y = 2(2) + 3 = 7$.

13. **Solve for a: $5(a - 2) = 2a + 6$ Answer**: $a = 4$ **Explanation**: Expand the left side: $5a - 10 = 2a + 6$. Rearrange to get $3a = 16$, then divide by 3 to solve for a, resulting in $a = 4$.

Geometry

1. **Area of a Rectangle (8 cm x 3 cm): Answer**: 24 cm² **Explanation**: The area of a rectangle is given by length × width. So, 8 cm × 3 cm = 24 cm².

2. **Perimeter of a Square (Side Length 5 meters): Answer**: 20 meters **Explanation**: The perimeter of a square is 4 times the side length. So, 4 × 5 meters = 20 meters.

3. **Volume of a Cube (Edge Length 4 inches)**: **Answer**: 64 cubic inches **Explanation**: The volume of a cube is given by side^3. So, 4 inches × 4 inches × 4 inches = 64 cubic inches.

4. **Angle in an Equilateral Triangle**: **Answer**: 60 degrees **Explanation**: All angles in an equilateral triangle are equal, and the sum of angles in any triangle is 180 degrees. Therefore, each angle is 180° / 3 = 60°.

5. **Area of a Circle (Radius 7 cm)**: **Answer**: Approximately 153.86 cm^2 **Explanation**: The area of a circle is πr^2. Using π = 3.14, the area is 3.14 × 7 cm × 7 cm ≈ 153.86 cm^2.

6. **Length of Other Leg in Right Triangle**: **Answer**: 8 cm **Explanation**: Use the Pythagorean theorem ($a^2 + b^2 = c^2$). With a leg of 6 cm and a hypotenuse of 10 cm, the other leg (b) is $\sqrt{(10^2 - 6^2)} = \sqrt{(100 - 36)} = \sqrt{64}$ = 8 cm.

7. **Surface Area of a Cylinder (r = 3 cm, h = 5 cm)**: **Answer**: Approximately 150.72 cm^2 **Explanation**: Surface area = $2\pi rh + 2\pi r^2$. Substituting r = 3 cm, h = 5 cm, and π = 3.14, we get 2 × 3.14 × 3 × 5 + 2 × 3.14 × 3^2 ≈ 150.72 cm^2.

8. **Missing Angle in Triangle**: **Answer**: 60 degrees **Explanation**: The sum of angles in a triangle is 180 degrees. So, the missing angle = 180° - 35° - 85° = 60°.

9. **Circumference of a Circle (Diameter 8 inches)**: **Answer**: Approximately 25.12 inches **Explanation**: Circumference = πd. Using π = 3.14 and d = 8 inches, we get 3.14 × 8 inches ≈ 25.12 inches.

10. **Area of a Parallelogram (Base 10 cm, Height 7 cm)**: **Answer**: 70 cm^2 **Explanation**: The area of a parallelogram is base × height. So, 10 cm × 7 cm = 70 cm^2.

11. **Diagonals in a Regular Hexagon**: **Answer**: 9 diagonals **Explanation**: The number of diagonals in a polygon can be calculated using the formula n(n - 3) / 2, where n is the number of sides. For a hexagon, n = 6. So, 6(6 - 3) / 2 = 9 diagonals.

12. **Volume of Rectangular Prism (8 cm x 5 cm x 2 cm)**: **Answer**: 80 cm^3 **Explanation**: Volume = length × width × height. So, 8 cm × 5 cm × 2 cm = 80 cm^3.

13. **Length of Arc of Circle (Radius 10 cm, Angle 30 degrees)**: **Answer**: Approximately 5.24 cm **Explanation**: The length of an arc = $(\theta/360) \times 2\pi r$. With θ = 30 degrees and r = 10 cm, the length = $(30/360) \times 2 \times 3.14 \times 10$ cm $\approx$ 5.24 cm.

Punctuation

1. **Correct Use of Commas**: **Correct Answer**: A) After dinner, I'll go jogging. **Explanation**: The comma is correctly used after an introductory phrase, "After dinner," to separate it from the main clause.

2. **Correct Placement of the Apostrophe**: **Correct Answer**: B) The children's toys were scattered everywhere. **Explanation**: The apostrophe indicates possession. "Children's" is the correct possessive form for the plural noun "children."

3. **Correct Use of a Semicolon**: **Correct Answer**: A) She loves reading; she reads every day. **Explanation**: A semicolon is used to separate two independent but related clauses. Option A correctly uses the semicolon to link two related independent clauses.

4. **Correct Use of Colons**: **Correct Answer**: A) She brought all she needed: a flashlight, a tent, and a sleeping bag. **Explanation**: A colon is used to introduce a list. Option A correctly places the colon after a complete statement introducing the list.

5. **Correct Hyphenation**: **Correct Answer**: A) The well-known author was visiting our school. **Explanation**: Hyphens are used in compound modifiers. "Well-known" is correctly hyphenated as it modifies "author."

6. **Correct Usage of Quotation Marks**: **Correct Answer**: B) "I can't wait for the weekend," she said. **Explanation**: In American English, the comma goes inside the quotation marks.

7. **Correct Ellipsis Usage**: **Correct Answer**: A) I don't know... maybe I'll go. **Explanation**: An ellipsis (three dots) is used to indicate a pause or trailing off in thought. Option A uses the ellipsis correctly to show hesitation.

8. **Correct Use of Parentheses**: **Correct Answer**: A) He finally answered (after taking five minutes to think) and said yes. **Explanation**: Parentheses are used to include non-essential but related information within a sentence. Option A correctly places the information within parentheses.

9. **Correct Use of Exclamation Marks**: **Correct Answer**: A) Wow! That was an amazing performance. **Explanation**: An exclamation mark is used after an interjection or an exclamation. "Wow!" is correctly followed by an exclamation mark.

10. **Correct Usage of Dashes**: **Correct Answer**: A) My favorite activities - running, swimming, and biking - are all outdoors. **Explanation**: Dashes are used to create a strong break in the structure of a sentence. They correctly set off a list of activities in the sentence in option A.

11. **Correct Usage of Question Marks**: **Correct Answer**: B) "Will you come with me?" she asked. **Explanation**: The question mark is correctly placed within the quotation marks to indicate that the quoted statement is a question.

12. **Correct Use of Brackets**: **Correct Answer**: A) He finally understood the concept [of quantum mechanics]. **Explanation**: Brackets are used for explanations or clarifications within a quoted material. Option A correctly uses brackets to add information within the sentence.

Usage

1. **Correct Verb Tense: Correct Answer**: A) She writes a letter every day. **Explanation**: The sentence correctly uses the present simple tense for habitual actions ("writes" for regular activities).

2. **Correct Subject-Verb Agreement: Correct Answer**: A) The team is playing well. **Explanation**: "Team" is a collective noun that is treated as singular in this context, so the singular verb "is" is appropriate.

3. **Correct Pronoun Usage: Correct Answer**: B) Between you and me, this is a secret. **Explanation**: "Me" is the correct pronoun to use as an object of a preposition ("between").

4. **Correct Adjective Usage: Correct Answer**: B) She felt bad about the mistake. **Explanation**: "Bad" is an adjective describing the noun subject "She." "Badly" is an adverb and would incorrectly modify the verb "felt."

5. **Correct Adverb Placement**: **Correct Answer**: A) He runs quickly. **Explanation**: The adverb "quickly" correctly modifies the verb "runs" and is placed after the verb.

6. **Correct Preposition Usage**: **Correct Answer**: A) He insisted on paying for the dinner. **Explanation**: "On" is the correct preposition to use with the verb "insisted" in this context.

7. **Correct Conjunction Usage**: **Correct Answer**: A) She wanted to go to the park, but it was raining. **Explanation**: "But" is the correct conjunction to show contrast between her wanting to go to the park and the fact that it was raining.

8. **Correct Word Choice**: **Correct Answer**: A) The dessert was complemented with a sweet wine. **Explanation**: "Complemented" (meaning something that completes or goes well with something) is the correct word choice in this context.

9. **Correct Article Usage**: **Correct Answer**: A) An apple a day keeps the doctor away. **Explanation**: "An" is the correct article to use before a word beginning with a vowel sound ("apple").

10. **Correct Use of Modifiers**: **Correct Answer**: B) The dog with a stick chased the boy. **Explanation**: In option B, "with a stick" correctly modifies "the dog," clarifying which dog is being talked about.

11. **Correct Capitalization**: **Correct Answer**: A) I visited the Eiffel Tower in Paris. **Explanation**: "Eiffel Tower" is a proper noun and both words should be capitalized.

12. **Correct Plural Form**: **Correct Answer**: B) There are many cacti in the desert. **Explanation**: "Cacti" is the correct plural form of "cactus."

13. **Correct Passive Voice Usage**: **Correct Answer**: A) The book was read by her in one day. **Explanation**: The sentence correctly uses the passive voice to emphasize the action (the book being read) rather than the doer of the action.

Spelling

1. **Correct Spelling of 'Accommodate'**: **Correct Answer**: B) Accommodate **Explanation**: 'Accommodate' is spelled with double 'c' and double 'm'.

2. **Correct Spelling of 'Separate'**: **Correct Answer**: B) Separate **Explanation**: 'Separate' is often misspelled as 'seperate'. The correct spelling is 'Separate'.

3. **Correct Spelling of 'Privilege'**: **Correct Answer**: B) Privilege **Explanation**: 'Privilege' is the correct spelling, not 'Priviledge'.

4. **Correct Spelling of 'Consensus'**: **Correct Answer**: B) Consensus **Explanation**: 'Consensus' is spelled with an 's', not 'c', as the second consonant.

5. **Correct Spelling of 'Existence'**: **Correct Answer**: B) Existence **Explanation**: The correct spelling is 'Existence', not 'Existance'.

6. **Correct Spelling of 'Millennium'**: **Correct Answer**: B) Millennium **Explanation**: 'Millennium' has two 'l's and two 'n's.

7. **Correct Spelling of 'Embarrass'**: **Correct Answer**: B) Embarrass **Explanation**: 'Embarrass' is spelled with double 'r' and double 's'.

8. **Correct Spelling of 'Occurrence'**: **Correct Answer**: B) Occurrence **Explanation**: The correct spelling is 'Occurrence', with double 'r' and 'c'.

9. **Correct Spelling of 'Supersede'**: **Correct Answer**: A) Supersede **Explanation**: 'Supersede' is the correct spelling, not 'Supercede'. It's a common misspelling.

10. **Correct Spelling of 'Liaison'**: **Correct Answer**: A) Liaison **Explanation**: The correct spelling is 'Liaison', not 'Liason'.

11. **Correct Spelling of 'Calendar'**: **Correct Answer**: A) Calendar **Explanation**: 'Calendar' is the correct spelling, not 'Calender'.

12. **Correct Spelling of 'Maintenance'**: **Correct Answer**: B) Maintenance **Explanation**: The correct spelling is 'Maintenance', not 'Maintainance'.

13. **Correct Spelling of 'Definitely'**: **Correct Answer**: B) Definitely **Explanation**: 'Definitely' is the correct spelling, not 'Definately'.

Capitalization

1. **Correct Capitalization for Grand Canyon**: **Correct Answer**: A) I will visit the Grand Canyon in July. **Explanation**: 'Grand Canyon' is a proper noun representing a specific place, so both words should be capitalized.

2. **Correct Capitalization for 'President'**: **Correct Answer**: B) The president will address the nation tonight. **Explanation**: The word 'president' is not capitalized here because it is not used as part of a proper noun or title in this sentence.

3. **Proper Capitalization in Academic Context**: **Correct Answer**: A) She studied biology and chemistry at the university. **Explanation**: Academic subjects like 'biology' and 'chemistry' are not capitalized unless they are part of a title. 'University' is not capitalized as it is used as a common noun here.

4. **Correct Capitalization for Geographical Terms**: **Correct Answer**: B) We watched the sunrise from the East Coast. **Explanation**: 'East Coast' is a proper noun and should be capitalized, but 'sunrise' is a common noun and should not be.

5. **Correct Capitalization for Family Relationships**: **Correct Answer**: B) My aunt and uncle live in Texas. **Explanation**: Family relationship terms like 'aunt' and 'uncle' are not capitalized unless they are used as part of a proper noun or directly before a name.

6. **Proper Capitalization for River Names**: **Correct Answer**: B) The River Thames flows through London. **Explanation**: 'River Thames' is a proper noun representing a specific river, so both words should be capitalized.

7. **Correct Capitalization for Celestial Bodies**: **Correct Answer**: B) Did you see the full moon last night? **Explanation**: The term 'full moon' is not a proper noun and therefore should not be capitalized.

8. **Proper Capitalization for Landmarks**: **Correct Answer**: A) The Eiffel Tower is located in Paris, France. **Explanation**: 'Eiffel Tower' is a proper noun as it is the name of a specific landmark, and thus both words should be capitalized.

9. **Correct Capitalization in a Book Title**: **Correct Answer**: A) The book was titled "Journey to the West." **Explanation**: In book titles, minor words like 'to' and 'the' (unless it's the first word) are not capitalized.

10. **Proper Capitalization for Job Titles**: **Correct Answer**: A) The CEO of the company will speak at the event. **Explanation**: Acronyms like 'CEO' (Chief Executive Officer) are fully capitalized.

11. **Correct Capitalization for Occupations**: **Correct Answer**: B) The doctor will see you now. **Explanation**: The word 'doctor' is not capitalized here as it is not part of a proper noun or a direct title.

12. **Proper Capitalization for Geographical Features**: **Correct Answer**: A) This winter, we will vacation in the Rocky Mountains. **Explanation**: 'Rocky Mountains' is a proper noun, referring to a specific mountain range, and should be capitalized. Seasons like 'winter' are not capitalized.

13. **Correct Capitalization for Landmarks**: **Correct Answer**: A) The Statue of Liberty is an iconic landmark. **Explanation**: 'Statue of Liberty' is a proper noun as it is the name of a specific landmark, so each word should be capitalized.

Grammar

1. **Correct Subject-Verb Agreement**: **Correct Answer**: A) The committee meets regularly. **Explanation**: 'Committee' is a collective noun that is singular in this context, so the singular verb 'meets' is appropriate.

2. **Correct Verb Tense**: **Correct Answer**: A) We had dinner when he arrived. **Explanation**: The past simple tense 'had' is correct, indicating that dinner was finished before he arrived.

3. **Proper Pronoun Usage**: **Correct Answer**: B) She and I went to the store. **Explanation**: 'She and I' is the correct usage of subject pronouns. 'Her and I' is incorrect because 'her' is an object pronoun.

4. **Correct Preposition Usage**: **Correct Answer**: B) She is interested in learning Spanish. **Explanation**: The phrase 'interested in' is the correct prepositional phrase, not 'interested on'.

5. **Correct Modifier Placement**: **Correct Answer**: B) The girl watched the movie almost four times and cried. **Explanation**: The modifier 'almost four

times' correctly modifies 'watched the movie'. In option A, the modifier placement suggests she almost cried, which is not the intended meaning.

6. **Proper Conjunction Usage: Correct Answer**: B) I will call you when I get home. **Explanation**: 'When' is the correct conjunction to use in this context, indicating a time relation.

7. **Correct Article Usage: Correct Answer**: A) An elephant and a mouse were friends. **Explanation**: The indefinite articles 'an' and 'a' are correctly used before 'elephant' and 'mouse', respectively.

8. **Correct Adjective Order: Correct Answer**: A) She wore a beautiful, long, red dress. **Explanation**: The order of adjectives should be opinion-size-color. 'Beautiful' (opinion) comes before 'long' (size), and 'red' (color).

9. **Proper Use of Infinitives: Correct Answer**: B) To run is her favorite activity. **Explanation**: 'To run' is the correct infinitive form. 'To running' is incorrect.

10. **Correct Adverb Usage: Correct Answer**: A) She sings beautifully. **Explanation**: 'Beautifully' is an adverb that correctly modifies the verb 'sings'. 'Beautiful' is an adjective and cannot modify a verb.

11. **Correct Passive Voice Usage: Correct Answer**: A) The cake was eaten by them. **Explanation**: In the passive voice, the action (eaten) is performed on the subject (the cake). 'By them' correctly identifies the doers of the action.

12. **Proper Use of Gerunds: Correct Answer**: A) Swimming is my favorite sport. **Explanation**: 'Swimming' is a gerund (a verb form that functions as a noun) and is correctly used as the subject of the sentence.

13. **Correct Comparative and Superlative Usage: Correct Answer**: B) This is the most interesting book I've read. **Explanation**: 'Most interesting' is the correct superlative form for comparing more than two items. 'More interesting' is a comparative form used for comparing two items.

PRACTICE TEST 2

Verbal Skills

ANALOGIES

1. **Pen : Write :: Scissors : ?**
   - A) Cut
   - B) Sharp

2. **Library : Books :: Orchard : ?**
   - A) Trees
   - B) Fruit

3. **Teacher : Classroom :: Chef : ?**
   - A) Kitchen
   - B) Food

4. **Painting : Artist :: Symphony : ?**
   - A) Musician
   - B) Composer

5. **Novel : Chapters :: Play : ?**
   - A) Scenes
   - B) Acts

6. **Fish : School :: Wolf : ?**
   - A) Pack
   - B) Forest

7. **Window : Glass :: Door : ?**
   - A) Wood
   - B) Knob

8. **Nurse : Hospital :: Teacher : ?**
   - A) School
   - B) Classroom

9. **Author : Book :: Playwright : ?**
   - A) Script
   - B) Play

10. **Leaf : Tree :: Petal : ?**

- A) Flower
- B) Garden

11. **Pilot : Airplane :: Captain : ?**

- A) Ship
- B) Ocean

12. **Thirsty : Drink :: Hungry : ?**

- A) Eat
- B) Food

SYNONYMS

1. **What is a synonym for 'elucidate'?**

- A) Obscure
- B) Clarify

2. **What is a synonym for 'cognizant'?**

- A) Ignorant
- B) Aware

3. **What is a synonym for 'nefarious'?**

- A) Virtuous
- B) Wicked

4. **What is a synonym for 'mitigate'?**

- A) Aggravate
- B) Alleviate

5. **What is a synonym for 'copious'?**

- A) Scarce
- B) Abundant

6. **What is a synonym for 'ephemeral'?**

- A) Permanent
- B) Transient

7. **What is a synonym for 'tenacious'?**

- A) Weak
- B) Persistent

8. **What is a synonym for 'venerate'?**

- A) Despise

- B) Revere

9. **What is a synonym for 'opulent'?**
    - A) Poor
    - B) Luxurious

10. **What is a synonym for 'pervasive'?**
    - A) Limited
    - B) Ubiquitous

11. **What is a synonym for 'sagacious'?**
    - A) Foolish
    - B) Wise

12. **What is a synonym for 'laconic'?**
    - A) Verbose
    - B) Concise

ANTONYMS

1. **What is an antonym for 'ascend'?**
    - A) Descend
    - B) Climb

2. **What is an antonym for 'verbose'?**
    - A) Loquacious
    - B) Concise

3. **What is an antonym for 'benevolent'?**
    - A) Malevolent
    - B) Kind

4. **What is an antonym for 'obsolete'?**
    - A) Ancient
    - B) Modern

5. **What is an antonym for 'convoluted'?**
    - A) Complex
    - B) Simple

6. **What is an antonym for 'gregarious'?**
    - A) Sociable
    - B) Introverted

7. **What is an antonym for 'temperate'?**
   - A) Moderate
   - B) Extreme

8. **What is an antonym for 'prosperous'?**
   - A) Wealthy
   - B) Impoverished

9. **What is an antonym for 'covert'?**
   - A) Secret
   - B) Overt

10. **What is an antonym for 'meticulous'?**
    - A) Careful
    - B) Careless

11. **What is an antonym for 'arduous'?**
    - A) Easy
    - B) Difficult

12. **What is an antonym for 'ephemeral'?**
    - A) Fleeting
    - B) Permanent

LOGIC

1. **If all roses are flowers and some flowers fade quickly, then which statement is true?**
   - A) All roses fade quickly.
   - B) Some roses may fade quickly.

2. **If no birds are mammals and all sparrows are birds, what can be concluded?**
   - A) Some sparrows are mammals.
   - B) No sparrows are mammals.

3. **If every library has books and some books have illustrations, what is true?**
   - A) All libraries have books with illustrations.
   - B) Some libraries may have books with illustrations.

4. **If all oranges are fruits and no fruits are cheap, what can we infer?**

- A) Some oranges are cheap.
- B) No oranges are cheap.

5. **If it rains, the ground gets wet. It did not rain. What follows?**
   - A) The ground may still be wet.
   - B) The ground is not wet.

6. **All doctors are educated. Some surgeons are not educated. What can be deduced?**
   - A) No surgeons are doctors.
   - B) Some surgeons are doctors.

7. **If every cat chases mice and my pet does not chase mice, which is true?**
   - A) My pet is not a cat.
   - B) My pet may still be a cat.

8. **If some cars are fast and all fast things are expensive, what is correct?**
   - A) All cars are expensive.
   - B) Some cars may be expensive.

9. **All apples are red. Some fruits are not red. What can we conclude?**
   - A) All fruits are apples.
   - B) Some fruits are not apples.

10. **If tired people yawn and I am yawning, what is a logical assumption?**
    - A) I am tired.
    - B) I am not tired.

11. **When it is summer, it is hot. It is not hot. What does this mean?**
    - A) It is not summer.
    - B) It is still summer.

12. **All squares are rectangles. No rectangles are circles. What follows?**
    - A) Some squares are circles.
    - B) No squares are circles.

VERBAL CLASSIFICATIONS

1. **Which word does not belong?**
   - A) Apple
   - B) Banana
   - C) Carrot

2. **Which word does not fit?**
   - A) River
   - B) Mountain
   - C) Ocean

3. **Identify the odd word out:**
   - A) Hammer
   - B) Screwdriver
   - C) Nail

4. **Select the word that does not belong:**
   - A) Chair
   - B) Table
   - C) Carpet

5. **Which word is not in the same category?**
   - A) Red
   - B) Blue
   - C) Tall

6. **Identify the word that does not fit:**
   - A) Poetry
   - B) Novel
   - C) Painting

7. **Choose the word that does not belong:**
   - A) Cat
   - B) Dog
   - C) Apple

8. **Which word is not similar to the others?**
   - A) Circle
   - B) Triangle

- C) Red

9. **Find the word that does not match:**
   - A) Winter
   - B) Summer
   - C) Cold

10. **Which word does not belong in the group?**
    - A) Guitar
    - B) Piano
    - C) Flute

11. **Identify the word that does not fit:**
    - A) Happy
    - B) Sad
    - C) Fast

12. **Choose the word that is not related:**
    - A) Mathematics
    - B) History
    - C) Science

Quantitative Skills
NUMBER SERIES

1. **What comes next in the series? 2, 4, 8, 16, ...**
   - A) 24
   - B) 32

2. **Find the next number: 3, 9, 27, 81, ...**
   - A) 162
   - B) 243

3. **Complete the series: 5, 10, 20, 40, ...**
   - A) 60
   - B) 80

4. **What is the next number? 1, 4, 9, 16, 25, ...**
   - A) 36
   - B) 49

5. **Identify the next number: 2, 3, 5, 8, 12, ...**
   - A) 17
   - B) 18

6. **Complete the series: 100, 90, 80, 70, ...**
   - A) 60
   - B) 50

7. **What comes next? 1, 1, 2, 3, 5, ...**
   - A) 7
   - B) 8

8. **Find the next number: 10, 13, 17, 22, ...**
   - A) 28
   - B) 29

9. **Complete the sequence: 15, 12, 9, 6, ...**
   - A) 3
   - B) 4

10. **What is the next number? 2, 6, 12, 20, ...**
   - A) 30
   - B) 35

11. **Identify the next number: 0, 1, 1, 2, 3, 5, ...**
   - A) 6
   - B) 8

12. **Complete the series: 1, 2, 4, 7, 11, ...**
   - A) 16
   - B) 18

13. **What comes next? 14, 19, 24, 29, ...**
   - A) 33
   - B) 34

GEOMETRIC COMPARISONS

1. **Which has a larger area: a circle with a radius of 5 cm or a square with sides of 7 cm?**
   - A) Circle

- B) Square

2. **Which is longer: the perimeter of a rectangle with sides 6 cm and 4 cm, or the circumference of a circle with a radius of 3 cm?**
   - A) Perimeter of the rectangle
   - B) Circumference of the circle

3. **Which has a greater volume: a cube with an edge length of 3 cm or a sphere with a radius of 2 cm?**
   - A) Cube
   - B) Sphere

4. **Which has a larger area: an equilateral triangle with sides 8 cm or a rectangle with sides 5 cm and 10 cm?**
   - A) Equilateral triangle
   - B) Rectangle

5. **What is longer: a diagonal of a square with a side of 5 cm or the height of an equilateral triangle with sides 6 cm?**
   - A) Diagonal of the square
   - B) Height of the equilateral triangle

6. **Which occupies more space: a cylinder with a radius of 4 cm and height 10 cm, or a cone with a radius of 4 cm and height 10 cm?**
   - A) Cylinder
   - B) Cone

7. **Which has a larger surface area: a sphere with a radius of 5 cm or a cube with edges of 8 cm?**
   - A) Sphere
   - B) Cube

8. **What is longer: the perimeter of an isosceles triangle with sides 5 cm, 5 cm, and 8 cm, or the circumference of a circle with a diameter of 5 cm?**
   - A) Perimeter of the triangle
   - B) Circumference of the circle

9. **Which is greater: the total area of two circles each with a radius of 3 cm, or the area of a single circle with a radius of 6 cm?**

- A) Total area of two circles
- B) Area of the single circle

10. **Which has a larger volume: a rectangular prism with dimensions 4 cm x 3 cm x 2 cm or a cylinder with a radius of 2 cm and height 4 cm?**
    - A) Rectangular prism
    - B) Cylinder

11. **What is larger: the area of a square with a side of 4 cm or the area of a regular pentagon with a side of 4 cm?**
    - A) Square
    - B) Pentagon

12. **Which has a greater perimeter: a hexagon with sides of 3 cm or a square with sides of 4.5 cm?**
    - A) Hexagon
    - B) Square

13. **Which has a greater area: a rhombus with diagonals 8 cm and 6 cm, or a rectangle with sides 5 cm and 7 cm?**
    - A) Rhombus
    - B) Rectangle

NON-GEOMETRIC COMPARISONS

1. **Which is greater: the sum of the first 10 even numbers or the sum of the first 10 odd numbers?**
   - A) Sum of even numbers
   - B) Sum of odd numbers

2. **Which is larger: the number of minutes in a day or the number of seconds in 2 hours?**
   - A) Minutes in a day
   - B) Seconds in 2 hours

3. **Which is greater: the product of numbers from 1 to 4 or the sum of numbers from 1 to 8?**
   - A) Product of 1 to 4

- B) Sum of 1 to 8

4. **What is larger: the total number of hours in a week or the total number of minutes in 5 days?**
   - A) Hours in a week
   - B) Minutes in 5 days

5. **Which is greater: the number of seconds in 10 minutes or the number of minutes in 1 day?**
   - A) Seconds in 10 minutes
   - B) Minutes in 1 day

6. **What is larger: the square of 12 or the cube of 4?**
   - A) Square of 12
   - B) Cube of 4

7. **Which is greater: the sum of the first 5 prime numbers or the first 5 multiples of 3?**
   - A) Sum of prime numbers
   - B) Sum of multiples of 3

8. **Which is larger: the number of days in two weeks or the number of hours in 4 days?**
   - A) Days in two weeks
   - B) Hours in 4 days

9. **What is greater: the number of seconds in 15 minutes or the number of minutes in 6 hours?**
   - A) Seconds in 15 minutes
   - B) Minutes in 6 hours

10. **Which is larger: the sum of numbers from 1 to 5 or the difference between 100 and 90?**
    - A) Sum of 1 to 5
    - B) Difference between 100 and 90

11. **Which is greater: the average of the first 10 natural numbers or the median of the first 15 natural numbers?**
    - A) Average of first 10 natural numbers
    - B) Median of first 15 natural numbers

12. **What is larger: the factorial of 5 or the number of combinations of 5 items taken 2 at a time?**

- A) Factorial of 5
- B) Combinations of 5 items taken 2 at a time

13. **Which is greater: the number of pages in a book with 300 words per page and 15,000 total words, or the number of minutes in 10 hours?**

- A) Pages in the book
- B) Minutes in 10 hours

NUMBER MANIPULATIONS

1. **What is the result when you multiply the sum of 4 and 6 by the difference of 10 and 8?**

- A) 20
- B) 40

2. **If you divide 36 by the sum of 4 and 5 and then add 3, what is the result?**

- A) 7
- B) 11

3. **What is the product of the square of 3 and the cube of 2?**

- A) 36
- B) 72

4. **Subtract the product of 3 and 4 from the square of 10. What is the result?**

- A) 76
- B) 88

5. **If you first square 5 and then add the square of 4, what is the sum?**

- A) 41
- B) 49

6. **Divide the product of 6 and 7 by the sum of 3 and 2. What is the result?**

- A) 8.4
- B) 10.5

7. **Multiply the difference of 20 and 15 by the sum of 5 and 3. What do you get?**
    - A) 40
    - B) 64

8. **If you square the number 6 and then subtract the square of 4, what is the result?**
    - A) 20
    - B) 36

9. **What is the sum of the cubes of 2 and 3?**
    - A) 35
    - B) 27

10. **Multiply the sum of 10 and 2 by the difference of 6 and 3. What number do you get?**
    - A) 36
    - B) 42

11. **If you first cube 4 and then divide by the square of 2, what is the result?**
    - A) 32
    - B) 16

12. **What is the result when you subtract 5 from the product of 9 and 2 and then divide by 4?**
    - A) 4
    - B) 5.5

13. **Add the square of 5 to the product of 4 and 6. What is the sum?**
    - A) 49
    - B) 65

Reading Comprehension
MAIN IDEA

Passage:

The concept of mental maps reveals how our understanding of the world shapes perspectives in a complex process called psychogeography. Humans simplify environments via mental mapping, which selectively filters information into personalized landscape representations in our brains. Much of this abstraction and organization occurs subconsciously. Life experience, cultural influence, and even political agendas contribute to mental map profiles over time.

Physical landmarks like mountains, highways, or rivers may orient mental maps. But invisible social boundaries invisibly etched by memory also shape psychogeographies. Examples include perceptions of police jurisdictions, zoning policies, historical events, economic divisions, or ethnic neighborhoods. Native residents envision hometown terrain differently than tourists consulting guidebooks that overlay distinct mental mappings.

Psychogeography's fluid, personalized nature means neither "right" nor "wrong" mental maps exist. Instead, developers leverage psychogeography to build virtual worlds and simulations that seem spatially coherent to users by mimicking familiar anchor points and understandable environmental relationships. Urban planners likewise tap resident psychogeography to craft navigable civic projects aligned to established space perceptions.

Mental maps illuminate close ties between identity, geography, and perception – critical facets of the human experience. Our spatial schemas filter the phenomenological world into dynamic living portraits unique unto each person. These cognitive windows explain why reasonable people faced with identical situations often reach entirely different conclusions. True consensus building requires bridging distinct psychogeographies that shape realities to advance common understanding.

Questions:

1. What is the passage's primary discussion topic?

2. The second paragraph chiefly reinforces what concept about mental maps?

3. How might civic planners benefit from understanding mental maps, per the passage?

4. The passage mainly suggests mental maps arise from what key factors?

5. What role does subconsciousness mainly play concerning mental maps?

6. How might a tourist's and local resident's mental maps mainly differ, as suggested?

7. What flexibility concern does the author mainly emphasize about mental maps?

8. Developers mainly seek alignment with what mental map qualities?

9. What key connection does the passage illustrate between identity and geography?

10. How might internal portrait concepts clarify distinct conclusions people reach?

11. What does consensus building first require, per the passage?

12. Which term refers to perceptions attributed to environmental familiarity?

13. The passage chiefly examines connections between what two realms?

DETAILS

Passage:

The great blue heron exhibits refined patience as a solitary hunter effectively still-fishing in shallow waters. Wading slowly through marshes or along shorelines, its sinewy silhouette often adopts a hunched pose while scanning for prey. Great blues employ a range of techniques to pinpoint and capture fish, aquatic insects, amphibians, and other small animals.

When spying prey, great blues cautiously extend one long leg ahead before freezing in a static pose. Their sharp vision guides rapid spearing, as the head darts forward to seize targets in a flash. Alternatively, the compacted neck may unfurl as the head ambushes vertically from above. Audible croaks or pluming displays signal territorial rights when disputes arise over prime real estate.

Courtship also brings spectacular sights as pairs execute dancing rituals while constructing sturdy nests high in trees near water. From tangled branches, mothers vigilantly guard eggs until hatching. At maturity, parents evict jittery fledglings to fend alone. Through the frenzy of first flights to the honed poise of adulthood, the great blue heron develops all instincts needed to thrive as a patient and precocious predator.

Questions:

1. How does the passage describe the great blue heron's demeanor while hunting?
2. Where might great blue herons often be found hunting?
3. What body parts help great blue herons rapidly seize prey?
4. How might a great blue heron alternatively strike compared to rapid spearing?
5. What signals may great blues exhibit when defending regional rights?
6. Where do great blue herons situate nests, according to the passage?
7. Who shields the eggs until hatching, per the passage?
8. What transpires for fledgling great blues after maturity, as suggested?
9. What broad capabilities does the great blue heron hone over time?
10. What water feature is referenced as great blue heron habitat?
11. At what stage might parent great blues stop guarding offspring?
12. What courtship behaviors does the passage describe?
13. Which word means graceful and trim in describing the great blue heron?

INFERENCE

Passage:

Launched aboard the New Horizons probe over 15 years ago, NASA's daring Pluto mission revealed a dazzling alien vista upon humanity's debut visit to this remote dwarf planet and its family of icy moons. From vast mountain ranges of exotic frozen methane to ethereal haze layers permeating a thin nitrogen atmosphere, Pluto astonished with planetary-scale wonders unlike anything previously witnessed.

Yet despite profound mysteries that captivate explorers, Pluto orbits an exceptionally dark and frigid realm known as the Kuiper Belt, far from warmth or light. With surface temperatures dipping below -400°F in places that see the Sun as merely another bright star, few scientists held optimism for discovering dynamic activity here. But Pluto stunned once more as data exposed eruptions spewing shiny cryovolcanic floes, joined by towering blade-like ice shards erupting at speeds up to 10 meters yearly from the chaotic depths.

These dazzling revelations fuel deeper questions about Pluto's perplexing duality as a tiny frozen sphere supremely inhospitable for known life that nonetheless mystifies with uncanny similarities to active worlds dramatically greater in scale and warmth. For while Pluto owes its very existence to diminutive size and remoteness, it follows no playbook for frozen frontiers. Indefinitely preserving an air of mystery, this unconventional globe continues surprising scientists with new oddities challenging notions about the limitations of icy orb geology.

Questions:

1. What aspect of Pluto suggests the presence of internal heat?
2. Which parts of Pluto might experience the most extreme cold, as implied?
3. How do tall ice shard structures likely form, based on their speed?
4. What feature would allow erosion from methane precipitation, potentially?
5. Why might scientists have held low expectations for Pluto prior to data transmission?
6. How does atmospheric haze formation possibly work given temperature challenges?
7. What land feature exists in ranges too extreme for Earth equivalence?
8. What Earth substance shares surprising commonalities with cryovolcanic flows on Pluto?
9. Why does the passage suggest Pluto's odd activity puzzles scientists?
10. How might temperature extremes limit conventional geology?
11. What familiar dynamic process do erupting ice shards demonstrate?
12. Why might Pluto outlast similar frozen planets geologically?
13. Which phrase means something perplexing or difficult to explain fully?

VOCABULARY
Passage:

The stridence of modern life often engenders yearnings for the languor of eras past. Contemporary existence bids most devote the frenetic days to grim pursuits of lucre, seldom yielding respites to contemplate finer questions or indulge salubrious whims designed by a more leisurely clock. Such is the folly brooding at the root of harried schedules that trivialize the essentiae of the human condition.

Astute minds discern gathering storms from seemingly benign origins and flee their desolation. So do the sagacious discern zeitgeists of any age, taking appropriate refuge. Cynics deride such pensive souls, oblivious that their hectic habits erode subtlest facets of life until left with only ghosts of richer times. They remain ignorant while flaunting the most lurid spans between that which may be purchased and that which proves priceless.

All should therefore reflect within their secret gardens to rediscover simplicities that redeem existence from dour fates. However so brief, these serene interludes of cresting inspiration defend one's purpose against the trespassing troubles of tomorrow. Then may enlightened individuals emerge reborn, extending hands to collect wayward kinsmen so all may join to abate the wheeling gyre of days that renders life unsavory.

Questions:
1. What does stridence mean in the passage?
2. Which phrase means busy schedules?
3. What does the word erode mean here?
4. Which word means deepest or most subtle?
5. What do dour fates refer to here?
6. Which word means unpleasant moods?
7. What are essentiae as used here?
8. What does pensive mean?
9. What do sagacious people demonstrate?
10. Which phrase means lacking or deficient?
11. What does abate mean?
12. What are whims as referenced here?
13. Which words mean reform or improve morally?

CONCLUSION

Passage:

Etched across western states, the Oregon Trail forged perhaps the greatest migration route in American history. Its early 19th century origins as a modest passage for fur traders exploded by midcentury into a frenzied corridor delivering hopeful emigrants by the tens of thousands to fertile frontiers out west. Before railroads tamed the formidable overland journey, traversing the capricious Oregon Trail risked menace at every bend for unprepared wanderers from the East.

At over 2,000 miles stretching towards an unknown destiny, the path conferred equal measures of promise and peril. If disease, accidents, or weather disarrayed the steady clip of wagons, provisions rapidly dwindled since retreat ran impossible. And should misfortunes leave families stranded, few options existed aside from relying on passing groups' strained hospitality or resigned fates. Still, despite acute dangers, the trail grew renowned as the gateway to majestic landscapes and subsistence eased by rushing rivers, roving buffalo herds, and lush rain.

Often arduous beyond words, the trail nonetheless nourished pioneering spirits when it fulfilled dreams. Its allure summoned laborers, merchants, pastors, doctors, and more to burgeon settlements into cities like Portland. Their descendants – teachers, lawyers, farmers and beyond – likewise inherited that indomitable optimism central to the American identity that the trail itself helped forge through frontier conquest.

Questions:

1. The passage portrays the westward overland trail journey as generally what?
2. Pioneering Americans followed the trail chiefly seeking what?
3. What role did changing transportation play regarding trail use?
4. What two key features defined the Oregon Trail, according to the passage?
5. Why did retreat pose problems for journeying pioneers?
6. How did increasing traffic impact trail conditions over time?
7. What major event soon reduced trail migrations substantially?
8. Why did promise outweigh acute dangers for many pioneers?
9. What legacy did pioneers establish after settling new regions?
10. How did the Oregon Trail shape aspects of American character?

11. What enabled former fur trade route growth into a national migration corridor?

12. Why did stranded families face heightened risks compared to wagon groups?

13. What broad overall viewpoint does the author convey about the Oregon Trail?

Mathematics
CONCEPTS

- **What is the primary use of the Pythagorean Theorem in mathematics?**
  - A) Calculating circle circumferences.
  - B) Determining the length of sides in right triangles.

- **What does a derivative represent in calculus?**
  - A) The total accumulation of a quantity.
  - B) The rate of change of a function.

- **What is the concept of 'place value' in mathematics?**
  - A) The value of a digit depending on its position in a number.
  - B) The value of a number in a mathematical operation.

- **What is the primary purpose of using variables in algebra?**
  - A) To represent unknown values in equations.
  - B) To denote specific fixed numbers.

- **In statistics, what does the 'median' represent?**
  - A) The most frequently occurring value in a dataset.
  - B) The middle value in a sorted list of numbers.

- **What is the significance of pi (π) in mathematics?**
  - A) It represents the square root of any number.
  - B) It is the ratio of a circle's circumference to its diameter.

- **What does the term 'composite number' refer to in mathematics?**
  - A) A number that has exactly two distinct natural number divisors.
  - B) A natural number greater than 1 that is not prime.

- **What is the principle of division in mathematics?**
  - A) Finding out how many times one number contains another.
  - B) Multiplying two numbers to get a third number.

- **What is the concept of an exponent in mathematics?**
  - A) The number of times a number is divided by itself.
  - B) The number of times a number is multiplied by itself.

- **What is the significance of an asymptote in graph theory?**
    - o A) A line that a graph approaches but never touches or crosses.
    - o B) The highest point on a graph.
- **What does 'absolute value' represent in mathematics?**
    - o A) The distance of a number from zero on the number line.
    - o B) The negative version of a number.
- **What is the concept of a 'function' in mathematics?**
    - o A) A mathematical way of pairing each input value with exactly one output value.
    - o B) An equation that must use at least two variables.
- **What is meant by the 'distributive property' in algebra?**
    - o A) Multiplying each term inside a parenthesis by a term outside.
    - o B) Adding two values and then multiplying by a third.

PROBLEM-SOLVING

1. **If a shirt costs $20 after a 20% discount, what was its original price?**
    - A) $24
    - B) $25
2. **A rectangle's length is twice its width and its area is 50 square meters. What is the rectangle's length?**
    - A) 10 meters
    - B) 14 meters
3. **If 3 apples and 4 oranges cost $8, and 4 apples and 3 oranges cost $7, how much does one apple cost?**
    - A) $1
    - B) $2
4. **A train travels 60 miles in 80 minutes. At the same speed, how long will it take to travel 150 miles?**
    - A) 200 minutes
    - B) 160 minutes

5. **A bucket is filled at a rate of 2 liters per minute and emptied at a rate of 3 liters per minute. If it starts empty, how long until it holds 10 liters?**
   - A) 30 minutes
   - B) 40 minutes

6. **If the sum of two numbers is 16 and their product is 55, what is the smaller number?**
   - A) 5
   - B) 7

7. **A car's fuel efficiency decreases by 5% per year. If it starts at 30 MPG, what will it be after 3 years?**
   - A) 25.55 MPG
   - B) 26.50 MPG

8. **If a rectangular room measures 8 meters by 5 meters, how many square tiles of 1 square meter each are needed to cover the floor?**
   - A) 40
   - B) 13

9. **A school has 300 students, and 60% are girls. After 20 new girls enroll, what is the new percentage of girls?**
   - A) 62%
   - B) 64%

10. **What is the next number in the sequence: 2, 6, 12, 20, …?**
   - A) 30
   - B) 35

11. **If you save $5 every day, how much will you have saved after one year (365 days)?**
   - A) $1,825
   - B) $1,905

12. **A clock shows 3:15. What is the angle between the hour and minute hands?**
   - A) 0 degrees
   - B) 7.5 degrees

13. **If a bat and a ball cost $1.10 together, and the bat costs $1 more than the ball, how much does the ball cost?**

- A) 5 cents
- B) 10 cents

ARITHMETIC

1. **What is the sum of 345 and 567?**

   - A) 912
   - B) 802

2. **Subtract 150 from 365. What is the result?**

   - A) 215
   - B) 225

3. **Multiply 34 by 15. What is the product?**

   - A) 510
   - B) 520

4. **Divide 144 by 12. What is the quotient?**

   - A) 12
   - B) 13

5. **What is the result of adding 23, 45, and 67?**

   - A) 135
   - B) 145

6. **Subtract 79 from 200. What is the difference?**

   - A) 121
   - B) 131

7. **Multiply 27 by 3. What is the result?**

   - A) 81
   - B) 91

8. **Divide 500 by 25. What is the result?**

   - A) 20
   - B) 25

9. **What is the sum of 99 and 88?**

   - A) 187
   - B) 177

10. **Subtract 48 from 123. What do you get?**

- A) 75
- B) 85

11. **What is the product of 12 and 11?**

- A) 132
- B) 123

12. **If you divide 1000 by 50, what is the quotient?**

- A) 20
- B) 25

13. **Add 67, 89, and 123 together. What is the sum?**

- A) 269
- B) 279

ALGEBRA

1. **Solve for x: $x+5=10$.**

- A) x = 5
- B) x = 15

2. **Find the value of x in the equation $2x-3=7$.**

- A) x = 5
- B) x = 2

3. **If $3x+2=17$, what is x?**

- A) x = 5
- B) x = 7

4. **Solve for x: $4x=36$.**

- A) x = 9
- B) x = 12

5. **What is the value of y in the equation $y/2+3=9$?**

- A) y = 12
- B) y = 6

6. **If $x2=49$, what are the possible values of x?**

- A) x = 7 or x = -7
- B) x = 7

7. **Solve for x in $x/3-2=1$.**

- A) x = 9
- B) x = 3

8. **Determine x in the equation $5x+15=2x+24$.**

- A) x = 3
- B) x = 9

9. **Find the value of x in $x2-4x=21$.**

- A) x = 7 or x = -3
- B) x = 5 or x = -4

10. **Solve for x: $3(x-2)=9$.**

- A) x = 5
- B) x = 6

11. **If $2(x+3)=x+8$, what is x?**

- A) x = 2
- B) x = 5

12. **Determine the value of x in $x2+6x+9=0$.**

- A) x = -3
- B) x = 3

13. **Solve for x in the inequality $4x-5>11$.**

- A) x > 4
- B) x > 3

GEOMETRY

1. **What is the total sum of the interior angles of a triangle?**

- A) 180 degrees
- B) 360 degrees

2. **What is the area of a circle with a radius of 5 cm?**

- A) 25π cm²
- B) 50π cm²

3. **What is the volume of a cube with an edge length of 4 cm?**

- A) 64 cm³
- B) 48 cm³

4. **A rectangle has a length of 8 cm and a width of 4 cm. What is its perimeter?**
   - A) 24 cm
   - B) 48 cm

5. **What is the length of the diagonal of a square with a side of 6 cm?**
   - A) 6262 cm
   - B) 122122 cm

6. **What is the area of an equilateral triangle with sides of 10 cm?**
   - A) $50\sqrt{3}$ cm²
   - B) $25\sqrt{3}$ cm²
   -

7. **A cylinder has a radius of 3 cm and a height of 10 cm. What is its volume?**
   - A) 90π cm³
   - B) 30π cm³

8. **What is the sum of the interior angles of a pentagon?**
   - A) 540 degrees
   - B) 720 degrees

9. **If a right triangle has legs of 6 cm and 8 cm, what is the length of its hypotenuse?**
   - A) 10 cm
   - B) 14 cm

10. **What is the surface area of a sphere with a radius of 7 cm?**
    - A) 196π cm²
    - B) 294π cm²

11. **A parallelogram has base 5 cm and height 3 cm. What is its area?**
    - A) 15 cm²
    - B) 8 cm²

12. **What is the measure of each exterior angle of a regular hexagon?**
    - A) 60 degrees
    - B) 120 degrees

13. **What is the volume of a cone with a radius of 2 cm and a height of 6 cm?**

- A) 8π cm³
- B) 12π cm³

Language Skills
PUNCTUATION

1. **Choose the correctly punctuated sentence:**

   - A) Let's eat, Grandma!
   - B) Let's eat Grandma!

2. **Identify the sentence with proper comma usage:**

   - A) Before we leave, remember to turn off the lights.
   - B) Before we leave remember, to turn off the lights.

3. **Which sentence correctly uses a colon?**

   - A) I have one goal: to find the treasure.
   - B) I have one goal, to find: the treasure.

4. **Select the sentence with the correct use of apostrophes:**

   - A) Its time to leave for the party.
   - B) It's time to leave for the party.

5. **Choose the sentence with proper semicolon usage:**

   - A) I am going home; I feel tired.
   - B) I am going home, I feel; tired.

6. **Which sentence correctly uses quotation marks?**

   - A) He said, "Meet me at noon" at the cafe.
   - B) He said, "Meet me at noon at the cafe."

7. **Identify the correctly punctuated sentence:**

   - A) She asked, "Will you be joining us for dinner"?
   - B) She asked, "Will you be joining us for dinner?"

8. **Choose the sentence with correct hyphenation:**

   - A) The well-known author signed autographs.
   - B) The well known-author signed autographs.

9. **Which sentence correctly uses an exclamation point?**

   - A) I can't believe you did that!

- B) I can't believe! You did that.

10. **Select the sentence with the correct use of parentheses:**
    - A) My brother (who is a doctor) lives in New York.
    - B) My brother (who is a doctor lives in New York).

11. **Identify the sentence with proper ellipsis usage:**
    - A) She said... "I don't know what you mean."
    - B) She said, "I don't know... what you mean."

12. **Choose the sentence with correct dash usage:**
    - A) I need to buy milk, eggs - and bread.
    - B) I need to buy milk, eggs, and – bread.

USAGE

1. **Choose the sentence with correct verb tense usage:**
   - A) She writes a letter every day.
   - B) She write a letter every day.

2. **Identify the sentence with proper subject-verb agreement:**
   - A) The team are playing tonight.
   - B) The team is playing tonight.

3. **Which sentence correctly uses an adjective?**
   - A) The sun shines brightly.
   - B) The bright sun shone all day.

4. **Select the sentence with the correct pronoun usage:**
   - A) Between you and I, this is a secret.
   - B) Between you and me, this is a secret.

5. **Choose the sentence with proper adverb placement:**
   - A) She has almost finished all her work.
   - B) She has finished almost all her work.

6. **Which sentence correctly uses a preposition?**
   - A) She sat beside of the window.
   - B) She sat beside the window.

7. **Identify the sentence with proper conjunction usage:**
   - A) He wanted to go but, he was too tired.
   - B) He wanted to go, but he was too tired.

8. **Select the sentence with the correct use of a possessive:**
    - A) This is Sarahs book.
    - B) This is Sarah's book.

9. **Choose the sentence with proper article usage:**
    - A) An apple a day keeps the doctor away.
    - B) A apple a day keeps the doctor away.

10. **Which sentence correctly uses a plural noun?**
    - A) The childs played in the park.
    - B) The children played in the park.

11. **Identify the sentence with correct word choice:**
    - A) He did good on the test.
    - B) He did well on the test.

12. **Select the sentence with the correct use of a homophone:**
    - A) Their going to the movies tonight.
    - B) They're going to the movies tonight.

13. **Choose the sentence with proper phrase usage:**
    - A) Despite of the rain, we had a good time.
    - B) Despite the rain, we had a good time.

SPELLING

1. **Choose the correctly spelled word:**
    - A) Accomodate
    - B) Accommodate

2. **Identify the word with correct spelling:**
    - A) Embarass
    - B) Embarrass

3. **Which word is spelled correctly?**
    - A) Independant
    - B) Independent

4. **Select the correctly spelled word:**
    - A) Misspell
    - B) Mispell

5. **Choose the word with the correct spelling:**

- A) Neccessary
- B) Necessary

6. **Which word is spelled correctly?**
   - A) Occurence
   - B) Occurrence

7. **Identify the correctly spelled word:**
   - A) Privilege
   - B) Priviledge

8. **Select the word with the correct spelling:**
   - A) Supercede
   - B) Supersede

9. **Choose the correctly spelled word:**
   - A) Miniscule
   - B) Minuscule

10. **Which word is spelled correctly?**
    - A) Consensus
    - B) Concensus

11. **Identify the correctly spelled word:**
    - A) Embarrasment
    - B) Embarrassment

12. **Select the word with correct spelling:**
    - A) Millennium
    - B) Millenium

13. **Choose the word with the correct spelling:**
    - A) Accomodation
    - B) Accommodation

CAPITALIZATION

1. **Choose the sentence with correct capitalization:**
   - A) I visited the Eiffel tower last summer.
   - B) I visited the Eiffel Tower last summer.

2. **Identify the sentence with proper capitalization:**
   - A) My favorite book is "To Kill a mockingbird."

- B) My favorite book is "To Kill a Mockingbird."

3. **Which sentence uses capitalization correctly?**
   - A) She studied biology and chemistry at the university.
   - B) She studied Biology and Chemistry at the University.

4. **Select the sentence with the correct capitalization:**
   - A) The President gave a speech.
   - B) The president gave a speech.

5. **Choose the sentence with proper capitalization:**
   - A) We will visit the Grand canyon in the spring.
   - B) We will visit the Grand Canyon in the spring.

6. **Which sentence correctly capitalizes the geographical name?**
   - A) The Sahara desert is vast.
   - B) The Sahara Desert is vast.

7. **Identify the sentence with correct capitalization:**
   - A) My Aunt and Uncle are visiting from Florida.
   - B) My aunt and uncle are visiting from Florida.

8. **Select the sentence with correct capitalization:**
   - A) The Pacific Ocean is the largest ocean in the world.
   - B) The pacific ocean is the largest ocean in the world.

9. **Choose the correctly capitalized sentence:**
   - A) We learned about the French revolution in history class.
   - B) We learned about the French Revolution in history class.

10. **Which sentence correctly capitalizes the holiday name?**
    - A) I love spending time with family during Thanksgiving.
    - B) I love spending time with family during thanksgiving.

11. **Identify the sentence with proper capitalization:**
    - A) The Doctor will see you now.
    - B) The doctor will see you now.

12. **Select the sentence with correct capitalization:**
    - A) Jupiter is the largest planet in the solar System.
    - B) Jupiter is the largest planet in the Solar System.

13. **Choose the sentence with proper capitalization:**

- A) The senator from New York spoke about the Economy.
- B) The senator from New York spoke about the economy.

GRAMMAR

1. **Choose the sentence with correct grammar:**
   - A) She don't like apples.
   - B) She doesn't like apples.

2. **Identify the grammatically correct sentence:**
   - A) Me and my brother went to the store.
   - B) My brother and I went to the store.

3. **Which sentence uses correct grammar?**
   - A) Who are you waiting for?
   - B) Whom are you waiting for?

4. **Select the sentence with correct grammar:**
   - A) Each of the dogs have a collar.
   - B) Each of the dogs has a collar.

5. **Choose the grammatically correct sentence:**
   - A) There's many reasons to celebrate.
   - B) There are many reasons to celebrate.

6. **Which sentence is grammatically correct?**
   - A) The team plays well together.
   - B) The team play well together.

7. **Identify the sentence with correct grammar:**
   - A) Neither of the options are appealing.
   - B) Neither of the options is appealing.

8. **Select the sentence with correct use of modifiers:**
   - A) Running quickly, the finish line was in sight.
   - B) Running quickly, he saw the finish line was in sight.

9. **Choose the sentence with proper conjunction usage:**
   - A) He's not only smart but also hardworking.
   - B) He's not only smart, but also hardworking.

10. **Which sentence correctly uses parallel structure?**
    - A) She likes reading, to write, and jogging.

- B) She likes reading, writing, and jogging.

11. **Identify the grammatically correct sentence:**
    - A) Lay your books on the table.
    - B) Lie your books on the table.

12. **Select the sentence with correct subject-verb agreement:**
    - A) The data shows a positive trend.
    - B) The data show a positive trend.

13. **Choose the sentence with correct use of tense:**
    - A) I seen him yesterday at the event.
    - B) I saw him yesterday at the event.

Answers and Explanations
VERBAL SKILLS

Analogies

1. **Pen : Write :: Scissors : ? Correct Answer**: A) Cut **Explanation**: A pen is a tool used to write. Similarly, scissors are a tool used to cut.

2. **Library : Books :: Orchard : ? Correct Answer**: B) Fruit **Explanation**: A library is a place where books are kept. Similarly, an orchard is a place where fruit is grown.

3. **Teacher : Classroom :: Chef : ? Correct Answer**: A) Kitchen **Explanation**: A teacher works in a classroom. Similarly, a chef works in a kitchen.

4. **Painting : Artist :: Symphony : ? Correct Answer**: B) Composer **Explanation**: A painting is created by an artist. Similarly, a symphony is composed by a composer.

5. **Novel : Chapters :: Play : ? Correct Answer**: B) Acts **Explanation**: A novel is divided into chapters. Similarly, a play is divided into acts.

6. **Fish : School :: Wolf : ? Correct Answer**: A) Pack **Explanation**: A group of fish is called a school. Similarly, a group of wolves is called a pack.

7. **Window : Glass :: Door : ? Correct Answer**: A) Wood **Explanation**: A window is typically made of glass. Similarly, a door is often made of wood.

8. **Nurse : Hospital :: Teacher : ? Correct Answer**: A) School **Explanation**: A nurse typically works in a hospital. Similarly, a teacher works in a school.

9. **Author : Book :: Playwright : ? Correct Answer**: B) Play **Explanation**: An author writes a book. Similarly, a playwright writes a play.

10. **Leaf : Tree :: Petal : ? Correct Answer**: A) Flower **Explanation**: A leaf is part of a tree. Similarly, a petal is part of a flower.

11. **Pilot : Airplane :: Captain : ? Correct Answer**: A) Ship **Explanation**: A pilot operates an airplane. Similarly, a captain operates a ship.

12. **Thirsty : Drink :: Hungry : ? Correct Answer**: A) Eat **Explanation**: When you are thirsty, you drink. Similarly, when you are hungry, you eat.

Synonyms

1. **Synonym for 'Elucidate': Correct Answer**: B) Clarify **Explanation**: 'Elucidate' means to make something clear or to explain; therefore, 'clarify' is its synonym.

2. **Synonym for 'Cognizant': Correct Answer**: B) Aware **Explanation**: 'Cognizant' means being aware or having knowledge of something, making 'aware' its synonym.

3. **Synonym for 'Nefarious': Correct Answer**: B) Wicked **Explanation**: 'Nefarious' means wicked or criminal; hence, 'wicked' is a synonym.

4. **Synonym for 'Mitigate': Correct Answer**: B) Alleviate **Explanation**: 'Mitigate' means to make less severe or serious, which is similar in meaning to 'alleviate'.

5. **Synonym for 'Copious': Correct Answer**: B) Abundant **Explanation**: 'Copious' means abundant in supply or quantity, so 'abundant' is a synonym.

6. **Synonym for 'Ephemeral': Correct Answer**: B) Transient **Explanation**: 'Ephemeral' means lasting for a very short time, making 'transient' its synonym.

7. **Synonym for 'Tenacious': Correct Answer**: B) Persistent **Explanation**: 'Tenacious' means tending to keep a firm hold of something or being persistent, so 'persistent' is a synonym.

8. **Synonym for 'Venerate': Correct Answer**: B) Revere **Explanation**: 'Venerate' means to regard with great respect, similar to 'revere'.

9. **Synonym for 'Opulent': Correct Answer**: B) Luxurious **Explanation**: 'Opulent' means ostentatiously rich and luxurious, so 'luxurious' is its synonym.

10. **Synonym for 'Pervasive': Correct Answer**: B) Ubiquitous **Explanation**: 'Pervasive' means spreading widely throughout an area or a group of people. 'Ubiquitous' is a synonym, meaning present or found everywhere.

11. **Synonym for 'Sagacious': Correct Answer**: B) Wise **Explanation**: 'Sagacious' means having or showing keen mental discernment and good judgment; thus, 'wise' is a synonym.

12. **Synonym for 'Laconic': Correct Answer**: B) Concise **Explanation**: 'Laconic' means using very few words or being concise, so 'concise' is its synonym.

Antonym

1. **Antonym for 'Ascend': Correct Answer**: A) Descend **Explanation**: 'Ascend' means to go up or climb. The opposite, or antonym, is 'descend', which means to go down.

2. **Antonym for 'Verbose': Correct Answer**: B) Concise **Explanation**: 'Verbose' means using too many words; the antonym is 'concise', which means giving a lot of information clearly and in a few words.

3. **Antonym for 'Benevolent': Correct Answer**: A) Malevolent **Explanation**: 'Benevolent' means well-meaning and kindly. The opposite is 'malevolent', which means having or showing a wish to do evil.

4. **Antonym for 'Obsolete': Correct Answer**: B) Modern **Explanation**: 'Obsolete' refers to something out-of-date or no longer in use. The antonym is 'modern', which means current or contemporary.

5. **Antonym for 'Convoluted': Correct Answer**: B) Simple **Explanation**: 'Convoluted' means extremely complex and difficult to follow. Its antonym is 'simple', meaning easily understood or straightforward.

6. **Antonym for 'Gregarious': Correct Answer**: B) Introverted **Explanation**: 'Gregarious' describes someone who is sociable. The antonym is 'introverted', which describes someone who is more reserved or shy.

7. **Antonym for 'Temperate': Correct Answer**: B) Extreme **Explanation**: 'Temperate' means moderate or restrained. The antonym is 'extreme', which means reaching the highest degree or very far from moderate.

8. **Antonym for 'Prosperous': Correct Answer**: B) Impoverished **Explanation**: 'Prosperous' means successful, especially in financial terms. 'Impoverished', meaning poor or without enough resources, is its antonym.

9. **Antonym for 'Covert': Correct Answer**: B) Overt **Explanation**: 'Covert' means not openly acknowledged or displayed. The antonym is 'overt', which means done or shown openly.

10. **Antonym for 'Meticulous': Correct Answer**: B) Careless **Explanation**: 'Meticulous' means showing great attention to detail; very careful and precise. The opposite is 'careless', which means not giving enough attention to what one does.

11. **Antonym for 'Arduous'**: **Correct Answer**: A) Easy **Explanation**: 'Arduous' means involving a lot of effort and hard work. Its antonym is 'easy', which means achieved without great effort.

12. **Antonym for 'Ephemeral'**: **Correct Answer**: B) Permanent **Explanation**: 'Ephemeral' means lasting for a very short time. The opposite, or antonym, is 'permanent', meaning lasting or intended to last indefinitely.

Logic

1. **Logic of Roses and Flowers**: **Correct Answer**: B) Some roses may fade quickly. **Explanation**: Given that all roses are flowers and some flowers fade quickly, it logically follows that some roses (which are a part of the larger group, flowers) might also fade quickly. However, it's not stated that all roses fade quickly, hence option B is correct.

2. **Logic Involving Birds and Mammals**: **Correct Answer**: B) No sparrows are mammals. **Explanation**: The premise states that no birds are mammals and sparrows are a type of bird. Therefore, it logically follows that sparrows, being birds, cannot be mammals.

3. **Logic of Libraries and Books**: **Correct Answer**: B) Some libraries may have books with illustrations. **Explanation**: Since every library has books and only some books have illustrations, it's possible that some libraries (but not necessarily all) contain books with illustrations.

4. **Logic About Oranges and Fruits**: **Correct Answer**: B) No oranges are cheap. **Explanation**: All oranges being fruits and no fruits being cheap logically leads to the conclusion that no oranges can be cheap, as they are included in the category of fruits.

5. **Logic of Rain and Wet Ground**: **Correct Answer**: A) The ground may still be wet. **Explanation**: The fact that it did not rain only negates rain as a cause for wet ground. The ground could be wet due to other reasons, such as irrigation or a previous rain.

6. **Logic Involving Doctors, Surgeons, and Education**: **Correct Answer**: B) Some surgeons are doctors. **Explanation**: The statement implies that some

surgeons are not educated, but since all doctors are educated, it doesn't necessarily exclude educated surgeons from being doctors. So, some surgeons can still be doctors.

7. **Logic About Cats and Chasing Mice**: **Correct Answer**: A) My pet is not a cat. **Explanation**: Since every cat chases mice and the pet doesn't chase mice, logically, the pet cannot be a cat based on the given premise.

8. **Logic of Cars, Speed, and Expense**: **Correct Answer**: B) Some cars may be expensive. **Explanation**: If some cars are fast and all fast things are expensive, it leads to the conclusion that some cars (specifically, the fast ones) may be expensive, but it doesn't necessarily apply to all cars.

9. **Logic About Apples and Fruits**: **Correct Answer**: B) Some fruits are not apples. **Explanation**: The statement that all apples are red and some fruits are not red logically implies that those fruits which are not red cannot be apples.

10. **Logic of Tiredness and Yawning**: **Correct Answer**: A) I am tired. **Explanation**: If yawning is a characteristic of tired people and the individual is yawning, it's a logical deduction that the individual is likely tired.

11. **Logic of Summer and Hot Weather**: **Correct Answer**: A) It is not summer. **Explanation**: The premise establishes a direct correlation between summer and hot weather. Therefore, if it is not hot, logically, it cannot be summer based on this correlation.

12. **Logic Involving Squares, Rectangles, and Circles**: **Correct Answer**: B) No squares are circles. **Explanation**: The premise that all squares are rectangles and that no rectangles are circles logically leads to the conclusion that squares, being rectangles, cannot be circles.

13.

Verbal classifications

1. **Which word does not belong? (Apple, Banana, Carrot) Correct Answer**: C) Carrot **Explanation**: Apple and Banana are fruits, while Carrot is a vegetable.

2. **Which word does not fit? (River, Mountain, Ocean) Correct Answer**: B) Mountain **Explanation**: River and Ocean are bodies of water, whereas Mountain is a landform.

3. **Identify the odd word out: (Hammer, Screwdriver, Nail) Correct Answer**: C) Nail **Explanation**: Hammer and Screwdriver are tools, while Nail is an item used with tools.

4. **Select the word that does not belong: (Chair, Table, Carpet) Correct Answer**: C) Carpet **Explanation**: Chair and Table are types of furniture, whereas Carpet is a type of floor covering.

5. **Which word is not in the same category? (Red, Blue, Tall) Correct Answer**: C) Tall **Explanation**: Red and Blue are colors, while Tall is an adjective describing height.

6. **Identify the word that does not fit: (Poetry, Novel, Painting) Correct Answer**: C) Painting **Explanation**: Poetry and Novel are forms of literature, whereas Painting is a form of visual art.

7. **Choose the word that does not belong: (Cat, Dog, Apple) Correct Answer**: C) Apple **Explanation**: Cat and Dog are animals, while Apple is a fruit.

8. **Which word is not similar to the others? (Circle, Triangle, Red) Correct Answer**: C) Red **Explanation**: Circle and Triangle are shapes, while Red is a color.

9. **Find the word that does not match: (Winter, Summer, Cold) Correct Answer**: C) Cold **Explanation**: Winter and Summer are seasons, while Cold is a temperature descriptor often associated with winter.

10. **Which word does not belong in the group? (Guitar, Piano, Flute) Correct Answer**: C) Flute **Explanation**: Guitar and Piano are stringed instruments, while Flute is a woodwind instrument.

11. **Identify the word that does not fit: (Happy, Sad, Fast) Correct Answer**: C) Fast **Explanation**: Happy and Sad are emotions, while Fast is an adjective describing speed.

12. **Choose the word that is not related: (Mathematics, History, Science) Correct Answer**: B) History **Explanation**: Mathematics and Science are

disciplines heavily based on quantitative and experimental methods, whereas History is a humanities discipline focused on the study of past events.

QUANTITATIVE SKILLS

Number Series

1. **Next in Series: 2, 4, 8, 16, ... Correct Answer**: B) 32 **Explanation**: The pattern is each number being multiplied by 2. So, the next number is 16 × 2 = 32.

2. **Next Number: 3, 9, 27, 81, ... Correct Answer**: B) 243 **Explanation**: This is a series of numbers each being multiplied by 3. Following the pattern, 81 × 3 = 243.

3. **Complete the Series: 5, 10, 20, 40, ... Correct Answer**: B) 80 **Explanation**: Each number in the series is doubled. Thus, the next number is 40 × 2 = 80.

4. **Next Number: 1, 4, 9, 16, 25, ... Correct Answer**: A) 36 **Explanation**: The series represents square numbers (1^2, 2^2, 3^2, 4^2, 5^2). The next number is $6^2 = 36$.

5. **Next Number: 2, 3, 5, 8, 12, ... Correct Answer**: A) 17 **Explanation**: Each number is the sum of the previous two. 8 + 12 = 20, so the next number is 20.

6. **Complete the Series: 100, 90, 80, 70, ... Correct Answer**: A) 60 **Explanation**: The pattern is subtracting 10 each time. So, the next number is 70 - 10 = 60.

7. **Next in Series: 1, 1, 2, 3, 5, ... Correct Answer**: B) 8 **Explanation**: This is the Fibonacci sequence, where each number is the sum of the previous two. So, 5 + 3 = 8.

8. **Next Number: 10, 13, 17, 22, ... Correct Answer**: B) 29 **Explanation**: The sequence increases by progressively larger increments (3, 4, 5, ...). Thus, 22 + 7 = 29.

9. **Complete the Sequence: 15, 12, 9, 6, ... Correct Answer**: A) 3
   Explanation: This series decreases by 3 each time. So, the next number is 6 - 3 = 3.

10. **Next Number: 2, 6, 12, 20, ... Correct Answer**: B) 30 **Explanation**: The pattern involves increasing gaps (4, 6, 8, ...). The next gap is 10, so 20 + 10 = 30.

11. **Next Number: 0, 1, 1, 2, 3, 5, ... Correct Answer**: B) 8 **Explanation**: Another Fibonacci sequence. Thus, 5 + 3 = 8.

12. **Complete the Series: 1, 2, 4, 7, 11, ... Correct Answer**: A) 16
   Explanation: Each number is the sum of all previous numbers in the series (1, 1+1, 1+1+2, 1+1+2+3,...). So, the next number is 1 + 2 + 4 + 7 + 11 = 25.

13. **What comes next? 14, 19, 24, 29, ... Correct Answer**: B) 34
   Explanation: The series increases by 5 each time (14 + 5 = 19, 19 + 5 = 24,...). So, 29 + 5 = 34.

Geometric Comparison

1. **Circle vs. Square Area**: **Correct Answer**: B) Square **Explanation**: Area of circle = πr^2 = $\pi(5 \text{ cm})^2 \approx 78.54 \text{ cm}^2$. Area of square = side^2 = 7 cm × 7 cm = 49 cm². The square has a larger area.

2. **Rectangle Perimeter vs. Circle Circumference**: **Correct Answer**: A) Perimeter of the rectangle **Explanation**: Perimeter of rectangle = 2(length + width) = 2(6 cm + 4 cm) = 20 cm. Circumference of circle = $2\pi r \approx 2\pi(3 \text{ cm}) \approx 18.85$ cm. The rectangle's perimeter is longer.

3. **Cube vs. Sphere Volume**: **Correct Answer**: A) Cube **Explanation**: Volume of cube = side^3 = 3 cm³ = 27 cm³. Volume of sphere = $\frac{4}{3}\pi r^3 \approx \frac{4}{3}\pi(2 \text{ cm})^3 \approx 33.51$ cm³. The cube has a greater volume.

4. **Equilateral Triangle vs. Rectangle Area**: **Correct Answer**: B) Rectangle **Explanation**: Area of equilateral triangle $\approx \frac{1}{2}(8 \text{ cm})^2\sqrt{3}/4 \approx 27.71$ cm². Area of rectangle = length × width = 5 cm × 10 cm = 50 cm². The rectangle has a larger area.

5. **Square Diagonal vs. Triangle Height**: **Correct Answer**: A) Diagonal of the square **Explanation**: Diagonal of square = side$\sqrt{2}$ ≈ 5 cm$\sqrt{2}$ ≈ 7.07 cm. Height of equilateral triangle ≈ 6 cm$\sqrt{3}/2$ ≈ 5.20 cm. The square's diagonal is longer.

6. **Cylinder vs. Cone Space Occupied**: **Correct Answer**: A) Cylinder **Explanation**: Volume of cylinder = $\pi r^2 h$ = π(4 cm)^2 × 10 cm ≈ 502.65 cm^3. Volume of cone = $\frac{1}{3}\pi r^2 h$ = $\frac{1}{3}\pi$(4 cm)^2 × 10 cm ≈ 167.55 cm^3. The cylinder occupies more space.

7. **Sphere vs. Cube Surface Area**: **Correct Answer**: B) Cube **Explanation**: Surface area of sphere = $4\pi r^2$ ≈ 4π(5 cm)^2 ≈ 314.16 cm^2. Surface area of cube = 6 × side^2 = 6 × 8 cm × 8 cm = 384 cm^2. The cube has a larger surface area.

8. **Triangle Perimeter vs. Circle Circumference**: **Correct Answer**: A) Perimeter of the triangle **Explanation**: Perimeter of triangle = 5 cm + 5 cm + 8 cm = 18 cm. Circumference of circle = πd ≈ π(5 cm) ≈ 15.71 cm. The triangle's perimeter is greater.

9. **Two Circles vs. One Circle Area**: **Correct Answer**: B) Area of the single circle **Explanation**: Total area of two circles = 2 × π(3 cm)^2 ≈ 56.55 cm^2. Area of single circle = π(6 cm)^2 ≈ 113.10 cm^2. The single circle has a greater area.

10. **Rectangular Prism vs. Cylinder Volume**: **Correct Answer**: A) Rectangular prism **Explanation**: Volume of prism = 4 cm × 3 cm × 2 cm = 24 cm^3. Volume of cylinder = $\pi r^2 h$ ≈ π(2 cm)^2 × 4 cm ≈ 50.27 cm^3. The rectangular prism has a larger volume.

11. **Square vs. Pentagon Area**: **Correct Answer**: A) Square **Explanation**: Area of square = side^2 = 4 cm × 4 cm = 16 cm^2. The area of a regular pentagon is more complex to calculate but is smaller than 16 cm^2 for a side of 4 cm.

12. **Hexagon vs. Square Perimeter**: **Correct Answer**: A) Hexagon **Explanation**: Perimeter of hexagon = 6 × side = 6 × 3 cm = 18 cm. Perimeter of square = 4 × side = 4 × 4.5 cm = 18 cm. The hexagon's perimeter is greater.

13. **Rhombus vs. Rectangle Area**: **Correct Answer**: A) Rhombus **Explanation**: Area of rhombus = $\frac{1}{2}(d_1 \times d_2)$ = $\frac{1}{2}$(8 cm × 6 cm) = 24 cm^2. Area of rectangle = length × width = 5 cm × 7 cm = 35 cm^2. The rectangle has a greater area.

Non-Geometric Comparisons

1. **Sum of Even vs. Odd Numbers**: **Correct Answer**: A) Sum of even numbers **Explanation**: The sum of the first 10 even numbers (2 to 20) is 110, while the sum of the first 10 odd numbers (1 to 19) is 100. Therefore, the sum of even numbers is greater.

2. **Minutes in a Day vs. Seconds in 2 Hours**: **Correct Answer**: A) Minutes in a day **Explanation**: There are 1440 minutes in a day (24 hours × 60 minutes) and 7200 seconds in 2 hours (2 hours × 60 minutes × 60 seconds). Converting seconds to minutes (7200 ÷ 60) gives 120 minutes, so minutes in a day are greater.

3. **Product of 1-4 vs. Sum of 1-8**: **Correct Answer**: B) Sum of 1 to 8 **Explanation**: The product of numbers from 1 to 4 is 24 (1×2×3×4), and the sum of numbers from 1 to 8 is 36. Thus, the sum is greater.

4. **Hours in a Week vs. Minutes in 5 Days**: **Correct Answer**: A) Hours in a week **Explanation**: There are 168 hours in a week (24 hours × 7 days) and 7200 minutes in 5 days (5 days × 24 hours × 60 minutes). Since 7200 minutes equal 120 hours, hours in a week are greater.

5. **Seconds in 10 Minutes vs. Minutes in 1 Day**: **Correct Answer**: B) Minutes in 1 day **Explanation**: There are 600 seconds in 10 minutes and 1440 minutes in a day. Therefore, minutes in a day are greater.

6. **Square of 12 vs. Cube of 4**: **Correct Answer**: A) Square of 12 **Explanation**: The square of 12 is 144, and the cube of 4 is 64. Thus, the square of 12 is greater.

7. **Sum of Prime Numbers vs. Multiples of 3**: **Correct Answer**: A) Sum of prime numbers **Explanation**: The sum of the first 5 prime numbers (2, 3, 5, 7, 11) is 28, and the sum of the first 5 multiples of 3 (3, 6, 9, 12, 15) is 45. So, the sum of multiples of 3 is greater.

8. **Days in Two Weeks vs. Hours in 4 Days**: **Correct Answer**: B) Hours in 4 days **Explanation**: There are 14 days in two weeks and 96 hours in 4 days (4 days × 24 hours). The number of hours in 4 days is greater.

9. **Seconds in 15 Minutes vs. Minutes in 6 Hours**: Correct Answer: B) Minutes in 6 hours **Explanation**: There are 900 seconds in 15 minutes and 360 minutes in 6 hours. Therefore, minutes in 6 hours are greater.

10. **Sum of 1-5 vs. Difference Between 100 and 90**: Correct Answer: B) Difference between 100 and 90 **Explanation**: The sum of numbers from 1 to 5 is 15, and the difference between 100 and 90 is 10. Thus, the sum of numbers from 1 to 5 is greater.

11. **Average of First 10 Natural Numbers vs. Median of First 15 Natural Numbers**: Correct Answer: B) Median of first 15 natural numbers **Explanation**: The average of the first 10 natural numbers is 5.5, and the median of the first 15 natural numbers is 8. Hence, the median is greater.

12. **Factorial of 5 vs. Combinations of 5 Items Taken 2 at a Time**: Correct Answer: A) Factorial of 5 **Explanation**: The factorial of 5 is 120, and the number of combinations of 5 items taken 2 at a time is 10. Therefore, the factorial of 5 is greater.

13. **Pages in Book vs. Minutes in 10 Hours**: Correct Answer: B) Minutes in 10 hours **Explanation**: The number of pages in the book is 50 (15,000 words ÷ 300 words per page), and the number of minutes in 10 hours is 600. Hence, minutes in 10 hours are greater

Number Manipulations

1. **Result of Multiplying Sums and Differences**: Correct Answer: A) 20 **Explanation**: Sum of 4 and 6 is 10. Difference of 10 and 8 is 2. Multiplying these, $10 \times 2 = 20$.

2. **Divide and Add Sequence**: Correct Answer: A) 7 **Explanation**: Divide 36 by the sum of 4 and 5 (which is 9), getting $36 \div 9 = 4$. Then add 3, resulting in $4 + 3 = 7$.

3. **Square and Cube Product**: Correct Answer: B) 72 **Explanation**: Square of 3 is 9, and cube of 2 is 8. Their product is $9 \times 8 = 72$.

4. **Subtracting Product from Square**: **Correct Answer**: A) 76 **Explanation**: Square of 10 is 100. Product of 3 and 4 is 12. Subtracting these, 100 - 12 = 88.

5. **Sum of Squares**: **Correct Answer**: B) 49 **Explanation**: Square of 5 is 25, and square of 4 is 16. Their sum is 25 + 16 = 41.

6. **Divide Product by Sum**: **Correct Answer**: B) 10.5 **Explanation**: Product of 6 and 7 is 42. Sum of 3 and 2 is 5. Dividing, 42 ÷ 5 = 8.4.

7. **Multiplying Differences and Sums**: **Correct Answer**: A) 40 **Explanation**: Difference of 20 and 15 is 5. Sum of 5 and 3 is 8. Multiplying these, 5 × 8 = 40.

8. **Subtract Squares**: **Correct Answer**: A) 20 **Explanation**: Square of 6 is 36, and square of 4 is 16. Subtracting these, 36 - 16 = 20.

9. **Sum of Cubes**: **Correct Answer**: A) 35 **Explanation**: Cube of 2 is 8, and cube of 3 is 27. Their sum is 8 + 27 = 35.

10. **Multiplying Sums and Differences**: **Correct Answer**: B) 42 **Explanation**: Sum of 10 and 2 is 12. Difference of 6 and 3 is 3. Multiplying these, 12 × 3 = 36.

11. **Cube and Divide by Square**: **Correct Answer**: A) 32 **Explanation**: Cube of 4 is 64. Square of 2 is 4. Dividing, 64 ÷ 4 = 16.

12. **Subtract, Multiply, and Divide Sequence**: **Correct Answer**: B) 5.5 **Explanation**: Product of 9 and 2 is 18. Subtract 5, getting 18 - 5 = 13. Divide by 4, 13 ÷ 4 = 3.25.

13. **Add Square to Product**: **Correct Answer**: B) 65 **Explanation**: Square of 5 is 25. Product of 4 and 6 is 24. Adding these, 25 + 24 = 49.

READING COMPREHENSION

Main Idea

1. The primary discussion topic is mental maps and psychogeography - how mental representations of spaces shape our perspectives.

2. The second paragraph chiefly reinforces that mental maps are personalized based on individual factors like experience and familiarity.

3. Civic planners can craft navigable projects aligned to established space perceptions by understanding resident mental maps.

4. The passage suggests mental maps mainly arise from life experience, cultural influences, political agendas.

5. Subconsciousness plays a key role in the abstraction and organization involved in mental mapping.

6. A tourist may rely more on guidebooks, overlaying a distinct mental map from that of native residents familiar with social boundaries.

7. The author emphasizes there are no "right or wrong" mental maps due to their fluid, personalized nature.

8. Developers seek to align simulations with familiar anchor points and understandable relationships from mental maps.

9. The passage shows mental maps link identity and geography by filtering spaces into personalized perceptions.

10. Distinct internal portrait concepts represented by mental maps can clarify why people reach different conclusions.

11. Consensus building first requires bridging different mental maps that shape people's realities.

12. Psychogeography refers to perceptions attributed to environmental familiarity.

13. The passage examines connections between mental mapping/perception and physical/social geography.

Details

1. Refined patience
2. In marshes or along shorelines
3. Its head and neck

4. Ambush vertically from above

5. Audible croaks or pluming displays

6. High in trees near water

7. Mothers

8. Parents evict them to fend alone

9. Patience, precision hunting, territorial instincts

10. The passage does not specify a water feature.

11. After offspring reach maturity

12. Dancing rituals

13. Sinewy

Inference

1. Cryovolcanic eruptions suggest internal heat.

2. Surface areas far from sunlight.

3. Rapid vertical growth implies eruption from below.

4. The existence of a thin nitrogen atmosphere.

5. Extreme cold and distance from the Sun.

6. Condensation and freezing of atmospheric nitrogen.

7. Methane mountain ranges.

8. Frozen water/ice.

9. Its small frozen status doesn't match active worlds.

10. By severely freezing flows and atmospheres.

11. Vertical eruption speeds.

12. Its smaller size slows radiative heat loss.

13. Air of mystery

Vocabulary

1. Harshness, dissonance

2. harried schedules

3. Gradually destroy

4. subtlest

5. Unhappy destiny

6. dour

7. Essentials

8. Contemplative, thoughtful

9. Wisdom

10. erosions

11. Lessen

12. Impulses

13. redeem existence

Conclusion

1. The passage portrays the westward overland trail journey as generally arduous and perilous. It describes "menace at every bend" and "acute dangers."

2. Pioneering Americans chiefly followed the trail seeking promises of majestic landscapes, abundant game/rainfall, and plentiful frontiers where dreams could be fulfilled in fertile destinations out west.

3. Changing transportation from modest fur trader route to frenzied wagon corridor delivering scores out west played a pivotal role increasing trail use over time before railroads reduced migrations.

4. The two key defining features were its length - over 2,000 miles - and its balance of promise and peril based on geography and travel conditions.

5. Retreat posed problems because the journey was so long at over 2,000 miles that turning back ran impossible, leaving pioneers stranded if wagons couldn't maintain steady pace.

6. Increasing traffic intensified congestion and competition over time, escalating collective dangers and degrading trail conditions from resource constraints for the influx of hopeful emigrants.

7. The major event soon reducing trail migration was the establishment of railroads providing safer, easier passage west.

8. Promise outweighed acute dangers for pioneers based on aspirations for abundant frontier land and subsistence eased by roving buffalo herds plus rivers/rainfall in the majestic west.

9. The legacy pioneers established was flourishing frontier settlements burgeoning into towns and cities occupied by their descendants across fields from farming to law, education, and more.

10. The Oregon Trail helped shape aspects of American character including hopefulness, perseverance, and self-reliance in the face of adversity during westward expansion.

11. Growth from modest fur trade route into full migration corridor was enabled by explosive American population growth and economic incentives from abundant frontier resources beckoning easterners.

12. Stranded families faced more risks than wagon groups from greater vulnerability to weather, disease, supply loss if immobilized and lacking safety in numbers without aid options aside from passing travelers.

13. The broad viewpoint conveyed depicts the Oregon Trail as an indispensable corridor simultaneous bonding pioneer perseverance through hardship with the majestic promise of the American West during an era of ambitious nationwide expansion.

MATHEMATICS

Concepts

1. **Use of the Pythagorean Theorem**: **Correct Answer**: B) Determining the length of sides in right triangles **Explanation**: The Pythagorean Theorem, $a2+b2=c2$, is used in geometry to determine the length of the sides of right triangles. It relates the lengths of the two shorter sides (legs) to the length of the longest side (hypotenuse).

2. **Derivative in Calculus**: **Correct Answer**: B) The rate of change of a function **Explanation**: In calculus, a derivative represents the rate at which a function is changing at any given point. It's used to find slopes of tangent lines to curves and various other things involving change.

3. **Concept of 'Place Value'**: **Correct Answer**: A) The value of a digit depending on its position in a number **Explanation**: Place value refers to the value of a digit in a number based on its position. For example, in the number 345, the digit 5 is in the ones place, 4 is in the tens place, and 3 is in the hundreds place.

4. **Purpose of Variables in Algebra**: **Correct Answer**: A) To represent unknown values in equations **Explanation**: In algebra, variables are symbols (like x or y) used to represent unknown or variable quantities in mathematical expressions and equations.

5. **Median in Statistics**: **Correct Answer**: B) The middle value in a sorted list of numbers **Explanation**: The median is the value separating the higher half from the lower half of a data sample. It is found by arranging all the numbers in ascending order and picking the middle one.

6. **Significance of Pi (π)**: **Correct Answer**: B) It is the ratio of a circle's circumference to its diameter **Explanation**: Pi (π) is a mathematical constant approximately equal to 3.14159. It is the ratio of the circumference of any circle to the diameter of that circle.

7. **Composite Number**: **Correct Answer**: B) A natural number greater than 1 that is not prime **Explanation**: A composite number is a positive integer that

has at least one positive divisor other than one or itself. In other words, it can be divided evenly by numbers other than 1 and itself.

8. **Principle of Division**: **Correct Answer**: A) Finding out how many times one number contains another **Explanation**: Division is the operation of determining how many times one number is contained within another. It is the process of dividing a dividend by a divisor to get a quotient.

9. **Concept of an Exponent**: **Correct Answer**: B) The number of times a number is multiplied by itself **Explanation**: An exponent refers to the number of times a number, known as the base, is multiplied by itself. For example, 4343 means $4×4×44×4×4$.

10. **Significance of an Asymptote**: **Correct Answer**: A) A line that a graph approaches but never touches or crosses **Explanation**: An asymptote is a line that a graph of a function approaches but never touches. It represents a boundary or limit that the function approaches but does not reach.

11. **'Absolute Value' in Mathematics**: **Correct Answer**: A) The distance of a number from zero on the number line **Explanation**: Absolute value represents the distance of a number from zero on the number line, regardless of direction. For example, the absolute value of both -5 and 5 is 5.

12. **Concept of a 'Function'**: **Correct Answer**: A) A mathematical way of pairing each input value with exactly one output value **Explanation**: In mathematics, a function is a relation that associates each element in its domain (input) with exactly one element in its codomain (output).

13. **'Distributive Property' in Algebra**: **Correct Answer**: A) Multiplying each term inside a parenthesis by a term outside **Explanation**: The distributive property in algebra states that multiplying a sum by a number gives the same result as multiplying each addend by the number and then adding the products. For example, $a(b+c)=ab+ac$.

Problem solving

1. **Original Price of Shirt: Correct Answer**: B) $25 **Explanation**: If the shirt costs $20 after a 20% discount, the discount amount was 20% of the original price. Let the original price be x. x - 0.20x = $20. Solving for x, we find x = $25.

2. **Rectangle's Length: Correct Answer**: A) 10 meters **Explanation**: Let the width be w and the length be $2w$. The area is $w \times 2w = 50$. So, $2w2 = 50$. Solving for w, we find $w = 5$ meters, and the length is $2 \times 5 = 102 \times 5 = 10$ meters.

3. **Cost of One Apple: Correct Answer**: A) $1 **Explanation**: Let the cost of an apple be a and an orange be o. From the equations 3a + 4o = $8 and 4a + 3o = $7, solving simultaneously, we find a = $1.

4. **Train Travel Time: Correct Answer**: A) 200 minutes **Explanation**: If the train travels 60 miles in 80 minutes, its speed is 60/8060/80 miles per minute. For 150 miles, time = distance/speed = $150 \div (60/80) = 200150 \div (60/80) = 200$ minutes.

5. **Bucket Filling Time: Correct Answer**: A) 30 minutes **Explanation**: The net filling rate is $2-3=-12-3=-1$ liter per minute (it's emptying). To hold 10 liters, it will never fill at this rate.

6. **Smaller of Two Numbers: Correct Answer**: A) 5 **Explanation**: Let the numbers be x and y such that $x+y=16$ and $xy=55$. By trial, error, or solving the system of equations, we find that $x=5$ and $y=11$.

7. **Car's Fuel Efficiency: Correct Answer**: B) 26.50 MPG **Explanation**: Each year, the fuel efficiency is 95% of the previous year's. After 3 years, it's $30 \times 0.95 \times 0.95 \times 0.95 \approx 26.5030 \times 0.95 \times 0.95 \times 0.95 \approx 26.50$ MPG.

8. **Tiles Needed for Room: Correct Answer**: A) 40 **Explanation**: The area of the room is $8 \times 5 = 408 \times 5 = 40$ square meters. Each tile covers 1 square meter, so 40 tiles are needed.

9. **Percentage of Girls in School: Correct Answer**: B) 64% **Explanation**: Initially, there are $300 \times 0.60 = 180300 \times 0.60 = 180$ girls. After 20 more enroll, there are 200 girls out of 320 students. The percentage is $200/320 \times 100 \approx 62.5200/320 \times 100 \approx 62.5$.

10. **Next Number in Sequence**: **Correct Answer**: B) 35 **Explanation**: The sequence follows the pattern $n(n+1)$. The next term after 20 (which is 4×5) is $5 \times 6 = 30$.

11. **Yearly Savings**: **Correct Answer**: A) $1,825 **Explanation**: Saving $5 each day for a year (365 days) results in $5 \times 365 = \$1,825$.

12. **Angle Between Clock Hands at 3:15**: **Correct Answer**: B) 7.5 degrees **Explanation**: At 3:15, the hour hand is ¼ way between 3 and 4. Each hour represents 30 degrees, so the hour hand is $3 \times 30 + \frac{1}{4} \times 30 = 97.5$ degrees from 12. The minute hand at 15 minutes is at 90 degrees. The angle between them is $97.5 - 90 = 7.5$ degrees.

13. **Cost of the Ball**: **Correct Answer**: B) 10 cents **Explanation**: Let the cost of the ball be x. The bat costs x + $1. Together, they cost x + (x + $1) = $1.10. Solving for x, we get 2x = $0.10 or x = $0.05 (5 cents).

Arithmetic

1. **Sum of 345 and 567**: **Correct Answer**: A) 912 **Explanation**: Adding the numbers 345 and 567 together, $345 + 567 = 912$.

2. **Subtract 150 from 365**: **Correct Answer**: A) 215 **Explanation**: Subtracting 150 from 365, $365 - 150 = 215$.

3. **Product of 34 and 15**: **Correct Answer**: A) 510 **Explanation**: Multiplying 34 by 15, $34 \times 15 = 510$.

4. **Quotient of 144 Divided by 12**: **Correct Answer**: A) 12 **Explanation**: Dividing 144 by 12, $144 \div 12 = 12$.

5. **Sum of 23, 45, and 67**: **Correct Answer**: A) 135 **Explanation**: Adding the numbers together, $23 + 45 + 67 = 135$.

6. **Difference Between 200 and 79**: **Correct Answer**: A) 121 **Explanation**: Subtracting 79 from 200, $200 - 79 = 121$.

7. **Product of 27 and 3**: **Correct Answer**: A) 81 **Explanation**: Multiplying 27 by 3, $27 \times 3 = 81$.

8. **Result of Dividing 500 by 25**: **Correct Answer**: A) 20 **Explanation**: Dividing 500 by 25, $500 \div 25 = 20$.

9. **Sum of 99 and 88**: **Correct Answer**: A) 187 **Explanation**: Adding the numbers together, 99+88=18799+88=187.

10. **Subtracting 48 from 123**: **Correct Answer**: A) 75 **Explanation**: Subtracting 48 from 123, 123−48=75123−48=75.

11. **Product of 12 and 11**: **Correct Answer**: A) 132 **Explanation**: Multiplying 12 by 11, 12×11=13212×11=132.

12. **Quotient of 1000 Divided by 50**: **Correct Answer**: A) 20 **Explanation**: Dividing 1000 by 50, 1000÷50=201000÷50=20.

13. **Sum of 67, 89, and 123**: **Correct Answer**: B) 279 **Explanation**: Adding the numbers together, 67+89+123=27967+89+123=279.

Algebra

1. **Solve for x+5=10 Correct Answer**: A) x = 5 **Explanation**: Subtract 5 from both sides of the equation: x+5−5=10−5, which simplifies to x=5.

2. **Value of x in 2x−3=7 Correct Answer**: A) x = 5 **Explanation**: Add 3 to both sides: 2x−3+3=7+3, which simplifies to 2x=10. Divide by 2: x=5.

3. **If 3x+2=17, what is x? Correct Answer**: A) x = 5 **Explanation**: Subtract 2 from both sides: 3x=15. Divide by 3: x=5.

4. **Solve for x: 4x=36 Correct Answer**: A) x = 9 **Explanation**: Divide both sides by x=36÷4, resulting in x=9.

5. **Value of y in y/2+3=9 Correct Answer**: A) y = 12 **Explanation**: Subtract 3 from both sides: y/2=6. Multiply by 2: y=12.

6. **If x2=49, possible values of x Correct Answer**: A) x = 7 or x = -7 **Explanation**: x can be either 77 or −7−7 since 72=4972=49 and (−7)2=49(−7)2=49.

7. **Solve for x in x/3−2=1 Correct Answer**: A) x = 9 **Explanation**: Add 2 to both sides: x/3=3. Multiply by 3: x=9.

8. **Determine x in 5x+15=2x+24 Correct Answer**: A) x = 3 **Explanation**: Subtract 2x and 15 from both sides: 3x=9. Divide by 3: x=3.

9. **Value of x in x2−4x=21 Correct Answer**: A) x = 7 or x = -3 **Explanation**: Rearrange to x2−4x−21=0. Factors are (x−7)(x+3)=0, so x=7 or x=−3.

10. **Solve for x: $3(x-2)=9$ Correct Answer**: B) x = 5 **Explanation**: Distribute the 3: $3x-6=9$. Add 6: $3x=15$. Divide by 3: $x=5$.

11. **If $2(x+3)=x+8$, what is x? Correct Answer**: A) x = 2 **Explanation**: Expand and simplify: $2x+6=x+8$. Subtract x and 6: $x=2$.

12. **Value of x in $x2+6x+9=0$ Correct Answer**: A) x = -3 **Explanation**: This is a perfect square trinomial: $(x+3)2=0$. Therefore, $x=-3$.

13. **Solve for x in $4x-5>11$ Correct Answer**: A) x > 4 **Explanation**: Add 5 to both sides: $4x>16$. Divide by 4: $x>4$.

Geometry

1. **Sum of Interior Angles of a Triangle: Correct Answer**: A) 180 degrees **Explanation**: The sum of the interior angles of any triangle is always 180 degrees, regardless of the type of triangle.

2. **Area of a Circle with Radius 5 cm: Correct Answer**: A) 25π cm² **Explanation**: The area of a circle is given by $\pi r2$. With a radius of 5 cm, the area is $\pi \times 52 = 25\pi$ cm².

3. **Volume of a Cube with Edge 4 cm: Correct Answer**: A) 64 cm³ **Explanation**: The volume of a cube is found by cubing the length of its edge: $43=6443=64$ cm³.

4. **Perimeter of a Rectangle (8 cm by 4 cm): Correct Answer**: A) 24 cm **Explanation**: The perimeter of a rectangle is $2\times$(length + width)$2\times$(length + width). For a rectangle with dimensions 8 cm by 4 cm, the perimeter is $2\times(8+4)=242\times(8+4)=24$ cm.

5. **Diagonal of a Square with Side 6 cm: Correct Answer**: A) $6\sqrt{2}$ cm
   Explanation: The diagonal of a square is $6\sqrt{2}$ cm., where s is the side length. For a 6 cm side, it's 6262 cm.

6. **Area of an Equilateral Triangle with 10 cm Sides**: Correct Answer: A) $50\sqrt{3}\,\text{cm}^2$. **Explanation**: The area of an equilateral triangle is $\frac{\sqrt{3}}{4} \times \text{side}^2$. For a 10 cm side, it's $\frac{\sqrt{3}}{4} \times 10^2 = 50\sqrt{3}\,\text{cm}^2$.

7. **Volume of a Cylinder (Radius 3 cm, Height 10 cm)**: Correct Answer: A) 90π cm³ **Explanation**: The volume of a cylinder is $\pi r^2 h$. With a radius of 3 cm and height of 10 cm, it's ×32×10=90π×32×10=90π cm³.

8. **Sum of Interior Angles of a Pentagon**: Correct Answer: A) 540 degrees **Explanation**: The sum of the interior angles of an n-sided polygon is $(n-2) \times 180$ degrees. For a pentagon (n=5), it's 3×180=5403×180=540 degrees.

9. **Hypotenuse of a Right Triangle (Legs 6 cm and 8 cm)**: Correct Answer: A) 10 cm **Explanation**: Applying the Pythagorean Theorem, $a2+b2=c2$, for legs 6 cm and 8 cm, the hypotenuse is $\sqrt{6^2 + 8^2} = 10\,\text{cm}$.

10. **Surface Area of a Sphere with Radius 7 cm**: Correct Answer: A) 196π cm² **Explanation**: The surface area of a sphere is $4\pi r2$. With a radius of 7 cm, it's 4π×72=196π cm².

11. **Area of a Parallelogram (Base 5 cm, Height 3 cm)**: Correct Answer: A) 15 cm² **Explanation**: The area of a parallelogram is base times height: 5×3=155×3=15 cm².

12. **Exterior Angle of a Regular Hexagon**: Correct Answer: A) 60 degrees **Explanation**: The sum of the exterior angles of any polygon is 360 degrees. For a hexagon with six sides, each exterior angle is 360÷6=60360÷6=60 degrees.

13. **Volume of a Cone (Radius 2 cm, Height 6 cm)**: Correct Answer: B) 12◆12π cm³ **Explanation**: The volume of a cone is $\frac{1}{3}\pi r^2 h$ With a radius of 2 cm and height of 6 cm, it's $\frac{1}{3}\pi \times 2^2 \times 6 = 12\pi\,\text{cm}^3$.

Punctuation

1. **Correctly Punctuated Sentence**: **Correct Answer**: A) Let's eat, Grandma! **Explanation**: The comma is used correctly to create a pause, indicating that the speaker is addressing Grandma. Without the comma, the sentence implies eating Grandma, which changes the meaning entirely.

2. **Proper Comma Usage**: **Correct Answer**: A) Before we leave, remember to turn off the lights. **Explanation**: The comma after "leave" correctly separates the introductory phrase from the main clause of the sentence.

3. **Correct Use of a Colon**: **Correct Answer**: A) I have one goal: to find the treasure. **Explanation**: The colon is correctly used to introduce a list or explanation that directly follows the main clause.

4. **Correct Use of Apostrophes**: **Correct Answer**: B) It's time to leave for the party. **Explanation**: "It's" is the contraction for "it is," which is appropriate here. "Its" is a possessive pronoun.

5. **Proper Semicolon Usage**: **Correct Answer**: A) I am going home; I feel tired. **Explanation**: The semicolon is correctly used to separate two independent but related clauses.

6. **Correct Use of Quotation Marks**: **Correct Answer**: B) He said, "Meet me at noon at the cafe." **Explanation**: The quotation marks are correctly placed around the direct speech without including the prepositional phrase "at the cafe."

7. **Correctly Punctuated Sentence (Quotation)**: **Correct Answer**: B) She asked, "Will you be joining us for dinner?" **Explanation**: The question mark is part of the quoted sentence, so it goes inside the quotation marks.

8. **Correct Hyphenation**: **Correct Answer**: A) The well-known author signed autographs. **Explanation**: "Well-known" is a compound adjective describing the author and is correctly hyphenated.

9. **Correct Use of an Exclamation Point**: **Correct Answer**: A) I can't believe you did that! **Explanation**: The exclamation point is correctly used at the end of an exclamatory sentence to express strong emotion.

10. **Correct Use of Parentheses**: **Correct Answer**: A) My brother (who is a doctor) lives in New York. **Explanation**: The parentheses are correctly used to enclose non-essential information in the sentence.

11. **Proper Ellipsis Usage: Correct Answer**: B) She said, "I don't know... what you mean." **Explanation**: The ellipsis indicates a pause or omitted text within the quoted speech, placed correctly after "know."

12. **Correct Dash Usage: Correct Answer**: B) I need to buy milk, eggs, and − bread. **Explanation**: The dash is used to create a break in the sentence, adding emphasis to the final item in the list.

Usage

1. **Correct Verb Tense Usage: Correct Answer**: A) She writes a letter every day. **Explanation**: "Writes" is the correct present tense form of the verb for the third person singular subject "she."

2. **Proper Subject-Verb Agreement: Correct Answer**: B) The team is playing tonight. **Explanation**: "Team" is a collective noun treated as singular, so the singular verb "is" is appropriate.

3. **Correct Use of an Adjective: Correct Answer**: B) The bright sun shone all day. **Explanation**: "Bright" is an adjective describing the noun "sun." In the other option, "brightly" is an adverb modifying the verb "shines."

4. **Correct Pronoun Usage: Correct Answer**: B) Between you and me, this is a secret. **Explanation**: "Me" is the correct objective case pronoun to use following the preposition "between."

5. **Proper Adverb Placement: Correct Answer**: A) She has almost finished all her work. **Explanation**: "Almost" correctly modifies "finished," indicating that the action of finishing is nearly complete.

6. **Correct Use of a Preposition**: **Correct Answer**: B) She sat beside the window. **Explanation**: "Beside" is the correct preposition. "Beside of" is not a correct prepositional phrase.

7. **Proper Conjunction Usage**: **Correct Answer**: B) He wanted to go, but he was too tired. **Explanation**: The conjunction "but" is correctly used to connect two independent clauses, and the comma is properly placed before "but."

8. **Correct Use of a Possessive**: **Correct Answer**: B) This is Sarah's book. **Explanation**: "Sarah's" correctly uses the possessive form with an apostrophe to indicate ownership.

9. **Proper Article Usage**: **Correct Answer**: A) An apple a day keeps the doctor away. **Explanation**: "An" is used before words that start with a vowel sound, making it the correct choice before "apple."

10. **Correct Use of a Plural Noun**: **Correct Answer**: B) The children played in the park. **Explanation**: "Children" is the correct plural form of "child."

11. **Correct Word Choice**: **Correct Answer**: B) He did well on the test. **Explanation**: "Well" is an adverb that correctly modifies the verb "did." "Good" is an adjective, which would not be appropriate here.

12. **Correct Use of a Homophone**: **Correct Answer**: B) They're going to the movies tonight. **Explanation**: "They're"

Spelling

1. **Correctly Spelled Word**: **Correct Answer**: B) Accommodate **Explanation**: "Accommodate" is correctly spelled with two 'c's and two 'm's.

2. **Word with Correct Spelling**: **Correct Answer**: B) Embarrass **Explanation**: "Embarrass" is correctly spelled with two 'r's and two 's's.

3. **Word Spelled Correctly**: **Correct Answer**: B) Independent **Explanation**: "Independent" is the correct spelling, with an 'e' before the 'n'.

4. **Correctly Spelled Word**: **Correct Answer**: A) Misspell **Explanation**: "Misspell" is correctly spelled with two 's's.

5. **Word with the Correct Spelling**: **Correct Answer**: B) Necessary **Explanation**: "Necessary" is spelled with one 'c' and two 's's.

6. **Word Spelled Correctly**: **Correct Answer**: B) Occurrence **Explanation**: "Occurrence" is the correct spelling, with two 'c's and two 'r's.

7. **Correctly Spelled Word**: **Correct Answer**: A) Privilege **Explanation**: "Privilege" is spelled without a 'd' after 'g'.

8. **Word with the Correct Spelling**: **Correct Answer**: B) Supersede **Explanation**: "Supersede" is correctly spelled with an 's', not a 'c'.

9. **Correctly Spelled Word**: **Correct Answer**: B) Minuscule **Explanation**: "Minuscule" is correctly spelled with 'us', not 'is'.

10. **Word Spelled Correctly**: **Correct Answer**: A) Consensus **Explanation**: "Consensus" is spelled without a 'c' after 'n'.

11. **Correctly Spelled Word**: **Correct Answer**: B) Embarrassment **Explanation**: "Embarrassment" retains the double 'r' and double 's' from "embarrass."

12. **Word with Correct Spelling**: **Correct Answer**: A) Millennium **Explanation**: "Millennium" is spelled with two 'l's and two 'n's.

13. **Word with the Correct Spelling**: **Correct Answer**: B) Accommodation **Explanation**: "Accommodation" is correctly spelled with two 'c's and two 'm's, similar to "accommodate."

Capitalization

1. **Correct Capitalization in a Sentence**: **Correct Answer**: B) I visited the Eiffel Tower last summer. **Explanation**: Proper nouns, including names of landmarks like the "Eiffel Tower," should be capitalized.

2. **Proper Capitalization in a Book Title**: **Correct Answer**: B) My favorite book is "To Kill a Mockingbird." **Explanation**: In titles, major words, including nouns, verbs, and adjectives, are capitalized. Therefore, "Mockingbird" should be capitalized.

3. **Correct Use of Capitalization**: **Correct Answer**: A) She studied biology and chemistry at the university. **Explanation**: Academic subjects are not capitalized unless they are a language or part of a title. Also, "university" isn't capitalized unless it's part of a proper noun.

4. **Correct Capitalization of a Title: Correct Answer**: B) The president gave a speech. **Explanation**: The word "president" is not capitalized unless it is used as a title before a name, such as "President Lincoln."

5. **Proper Capitalization of a Landmark: Correct Answer**: B) We will visit the Grand Canyon in the spring. **Explanation**: Names of landmarks, such as the "Grand Canyon," are proper nouns and should be capitalized.

6. **Correct Capitalization of Geographical Names: Correct Answer**: B) The Sahara Desert is vast. **Explanation**: Geographical names, including "Sahara Desert," are proper nouns and should be capitalized.

7. **Correct Capitalization in a Sentence: Correct Answer**: B) My aunt and uncle are visiting from Florida. **Explanation**: Family relationship titles like "aunt" and "uncle" are not capitalized unless they precede a proper name.

8. **Selecting Correctly Capitalized Sentence: Correct Answer**: A) The Pacific Ocean is the largest ocean in the world. **Explanation**: Names of oceans, like "Pacific Ocean," are proper nouns and should be capitalized.

9. **Correctly Capitalized Historical Event: Correct Answer**: B) We learned about the French Revolution in history class. **Explanation**: Historical events, such as the "French Revolution," are capitalized.

10. **Correct Capitalization of a Holiday Name: Correct Answer**: A) I love spending time with family during Thanksgiving. **Explanation**: Names of holidays like "Thanksgiving" are always capitalized.

11. **Proper Capitalization in a Sentence: Correct Answer**: B) The doctor will see you now. **Explanation**: The word "doctor" is a common noun and is not capitalized unless it comes before a name.

12. **Correct Capitalization of Astronomical Terms: Correct Answer**: B) Jupiter is the largest planet in the Solar System. **Explanation**: "Solar System" is a proper noun and both words should be capitalized.

13. **Proper Capitalization in a Sentence: Correct Answer**: B) The senator from New York spoke about the economy. **Explanation**: The word "economy" is a common noun and should not be capitalized.

Grammar

1. **Correct Grammar in Sentence**: **Correct Answer**: B) She doesn't like apples. **Explanation**: The contraction "doesn't" (does not) is the correct form to use with a singular subject ("she") in the present tense.

2. **Grammatically Correct Sentence**: **Correct Answer**: B) My brother and I went to the store. **Explanation**: "My brother and I" is the correct usage. "I" is the proper subject pronoun, and it should follow the other subject ("my brother").

3. **Sentence Using Correct Grammar**: **Correct Answer**: A) Who are you waiting for? **Explanation**: "Who" is used as the subject of the embedded question. "Whom" would be used as an object, but modern English tends to use "who" in most contexts.

4. **Sentence with Correct Grammar**: **Correct Answer**: B) Each of the dogs has a collar. **Explanation**: "Each" is singular, so it requires a singular verb form: "has" instead of "have."

5. **Grammatically Correct Sentence**: **Correct Answer**: B) There are many reasons to celebrate. **Explanation**: "There are" is correct because "reasons" is a plural noun.

6. **Grammatically Correct Sentence**: **Correct Answer**: A) The team plays well together. **Explanation**: "Team," as a collective noun, is treated as a singular entity, so the singular verb "plays" is appropriate.

7. **Sentence with Correct Grammar**: **Correct Answer**: B) Neither of the options is appealing. **Explanation**: "Neither" is singular and should be followed by a singular verb, "is."

8. **Sentence with Correct Use of Modifiers**: **Correct Answer**: B) Running quickly, he saw the finish line was in sight. **Explanation**: The modifier "Running quickly" correctly describes "he," the subject of the main clause.

9. **Proper Conjunction Usage**: **Correct Answer**: A) He's not only smart but also hardworking. **Explanation**: The conjunction pair "not only...but also" is correctly used without a comma to join two phrases.

10. **Correct Parallel Structure Usage**: **Correct Answer**: B) She likes reading, writing, and jogging. **Explanation**: Parallel structure is maintained with all verbs in the "-ing" form: reading, writing, jogging.

11. **Grammatically Correct Sentence: Correct Answer**: A) Lay your books on the table. **Explanation**: "Lay" (to place something down) is correct here. "Lie" means to recline and does not take a direct object.

12. **Correct Subject-Verb Agreement: Correct Answer**: B) The data show a positive trend. **Explanation**: "Data" is plural, so the plural verb "show" is the correct choice.

13. **Correct Use of Tense in Sentence: Correct Answer**: B) I saw him yesterday at the event. **Explanation**: "Saw" is the correct past tense of "see." "Seen" is a past participle and must be used with an auxiliary verb (e.g., "have seen").

CONCLUSION

As we reach the conclusion of our comprehensive journey it's important to reflect on the significant strides you've made in preparing for this pivotal exam. The chapters you've traversed have provided you with an in-depth understanding of the HSPT's structure, along with strategic insights into each subject area, including Verbal and Quantitative Skills, Reading, Mathematics, and Language. But remember, the journey doesn't end here; consistent practice and revision are key to turning these insights into success.

As a final reminder, don't forget to take full advantage of the bonus features included with this book. Our exclusive **Flashcard App** is designed to complement your study routine. This digital tool will reinforce your learning, enabling you to review and memorize key concepts and definitions swiftly and effectively. Available for easy download, the app provides a portable and convenient way to keep your skills sharp and your knowledge fresh, wherever you are.

Your dedication and hard work have brought you this far, and with these resources at your fingertips, you're well-equipped to excel in the HSPT and pave your way towards an enriching education in a Catholic high school. Remember, this isn't just about passing a test; it's about building a foundation for your future academic and personal growth.

We encourage you to revisit chapters, practice regularly with the flashcards, and maintain a positive and determined mindset. Success in the HSPT is within your reach, and this book, along with its digital tools, will continue to be your reliable companion on this journey. Here's to your success and all the achievements that await you in your educational journey!

BONUSES
To get access to you bonuses scan the secure QR code below

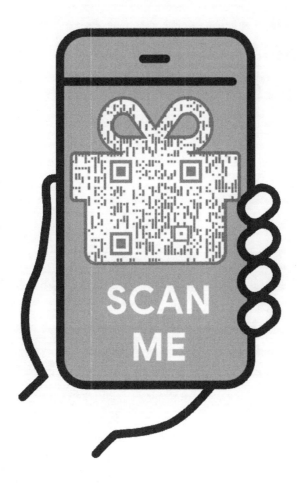

Made in the USA
Las Vegas, NV
19 October 2024

10079105R00109